PRAISE FOR *OUTSTANDING TEACHING: ENGAGING LEARNERS*

There are ma⸺ ⸺ ... and some of them are recognised. Most teachers would
seek to be th⸺ ⸺ to help the pupils that they teach become the learners we
would want t⸺ ⸺ help t⸺ ⸺gether the art, the science and the
craft of teach⸺ ⸺ work they do alongside teachers on
their course ⸺ LIB⸺ ⸺ and practical: no mean achievement!
It is a book fu⸺   Water Street, St Helens.⸺ ⸺unded in a coherent outlook on
what makes ⸺   **This book is due for re**⸺ ⸺spection ... and it is much more. Reading this
book will she⸺   ⸺⸺ms and the way we engage with youngsters –
and will also ⸺ ⸺se of teaching.

Mick Wate⸺, Professor of Education at Wolverhampton University

Books in education tend to be dry academic tomes or full of anecdotes usually premised on "do
what I did". Outstanding Teaching is neither – it is based on a rich analysis of thousands of videos of
successful teachers, is imbued with a sense of fun, but has some very serious messages.

What a treat – *Outstanding Teaching* an engaging book emphasising the core qualities of teaching
while making it sound fun. Griffith and Burns emphasise the Big Four; Challenge, Autonomy (but
they mean students having the space in classrooms to learn), feedback (to teachers), and engagement (full absorption in learning). To link these, they use the notion of flow, which requires that the
tasks are appropriately challenging, teacher input is minimal, the class have the necessary learning
skills, success criteria or goals are clear and worthwhile, feedback is immediate, and tasks are intrinsically motivating. These are among the top influences that I also found in my synthesis of
meta-analyses.

Many have become upset with my own comments about the power of teacher quality, so if only
they read this book to see what quality looks and feels like. They spare no punches about what is in
the power of teachers: not only the choice of curricula but the management of classrooms, the skill
of listening not speaking, the placing of student learning at the centre, receiving feedback about
their impact, and taking responsibility for triggering engagement by students in learning – whilst
enjoying it all. They emphasise rapport, imagination, competence, choice, curiosity, relevance, challenge, and fun. [With two exceptions I agree (I see little evidence supporting student choice – teachers
need to lead in progressing students upwards in their learning and not leave it to students other-
wise the rich can get richer and the poor stay poor) and would argue that some of these triggers
come from being successfully engaged (not as precursors to successful engagement).]

John Hattie, Director, Melbourne Education Research Institute

Steeped in the real-world exigencies of classroom life, yet also respectful of the theoretical models that underpin high-quality learning, this is an admirable book. Being much more than another compendium of engaging lesson ideas, *Outstanding Teaching* relates these hands-on ideas to a conceptually neat framework for promoting outstanding teaching and learning. Joe Renzulli taught us that hands-on needn't mean brains-off, and it certainly doesn't here. The authors have distilled their years of experience in and around classrooms into an easily-accessible and usable text. When motivation meets empowerment, shift happens. This book will generate shift.

Barry J Hymer, Professor of Psychology in Education, Education Faculty, University of Cumbria

Cutting through the complexities of the classroom with a well-evidenced and researched set of level performance descriptors (ones which Ofsted would do well to look at), Andy Griffith and Mark Burns provide themselves with a platform on which the rest of the book is based. Each chapter offers an appropriate balance of research and practical tips, meaning that not only are you working with ideas that generate outstanding learning in the classroom, but that you will also understand why they work – so you can go on and develop more ideas yourself. The encouragement given to reflect on your own performance as a teacher is well supported with numerous techniques and strategies, with the reader getting a sense that the authors have benefited themselves from reflection in their own classroom and therefore are justifiably passionate about how this helps achieve excellence. And it is that commitment to excellence that perhaps is the overriding tone of the book. So whilst the authors point out that there are no money-back guarantees if outstanding learning is not the outcome as a result of reading this book, I doubt very much that anyone will need a refund. Quite the opposite. They will be recommending it to a colleague. Just like I have.

Jim Smith Senior Leader and Author of *The Lazy Teachers Handbook*

The magic of this book is the motivational way in which it is written. Teachers cannot fail to be engaged by its down-to-earth style. The instant classroom tips which professionals can gain are evident on each and every page. I especially liked the FAQ sections and the direct links to additional information in each chapter. All teachers want to motivate, inspire and challenge young people. This book provides tips and skills to enhance every teacher's classroom practice. A great and practical read!

Anne Pontifex, Head Teacher, St John Bosco Arts College

Outstanding Teaching reflects Andy and Mark's views that all teachers can be enabled to improve with the right support and guidance that is tied to clear criteria that allows them to see how to move forward. The strength of the book comes from the number of strategies that are included, alongside real-life examples that can support classroom teachers in engaging students. To learn, students have to be engaged – this book gives a route map of what engagement is, what it looks like and the strategies needed to achieve it. Teachers need to do this before anything else, such as learning and progress, can happen in classrooms – this is what makes this book a valuable tool to classroom teachers.

Ian Young, Principal, Rainford High Technology College

OUTSTANDING TEACHING

ENGAGING LEARNERS

OSIRIS
EDUCATIONAL

THE OUTSTANDING
TEACHING SERIES

ANDY GRIFFITH
AND MARK BURNS

Crown House Publishing Limited
www.crownhouse.co.uk
www.crownhousepublishing.com

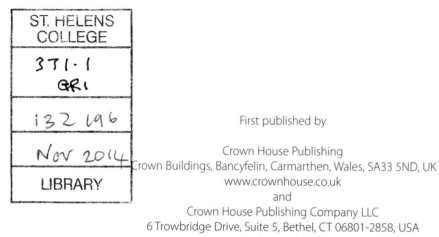
First published by

Crown House Publishing
Crown Buildings, Bancyfelin, Carmarthen, Wales, SA33 5ND, UK
www.crownhouse.co.uk
and
Crown House Publishing Company LLC
6 Trowbridge Drive, Suite 5, Bethel, CT 06801-2858, USA
www.crownhousepublishing.com

British Library Cataloguing-in-Publication Data
A catalogue entry for this book is available
from the British Library.

Print ISBN 978-184590797-6
Mobi ISBN 978-184590823-2
ePub ISBN 978-184590824-9

LCCN 2011946025

Edited by Nick Owen

Printed and bound in the UK by
Gomer Press, Llandysul, Ceredigion

To Joe, Anna, Gracie May and Ruby Rose

CONTENTS

ACKNOWLEDGEMENTS

Andy Griffith:

Firstly thanks to my Mum, Barbara, who took me to libraries and brought home comics such as *Look and Learn*, *World of Wonder* and supported me all through my education.

Thanks to my wife Clair, without her support, patience and good humour I would not have been able to build my career or write this book.

Thanks to the Labour government that created much maligned comprehensive education. The schools I went to were fantastic.

My first head of department was Ian Macleod. He helped me more than anybody to become a half-decent teacher. I am eternally grateful to you.

Thank you to my hard working colleagues who have shared their time, ideas and resources. I have learned a lot from you.

For support with writing and research and keeping me sane(ish) thanks, in no particular order, to Nick Owen, Caroline Lenton, Carol Williams, Anne Riley, Mark Blackburn, Tony McGuinness and Stephen Cox.

Mark Burns:

Thanks to my wife Kerry for her patience during the writing of this book. Thanks to my parents and family for nurturing my love of learning. Thanks finally to all of the fantastic, creative, passionate and hardworking teachers I've had the pleasure and privilege to work with and learn from.

FOREWORD

I believe that through high-quality training input, teachers and school leaders will improve, and the impact this produces will be felt directly in the classroom through the improved performance and better life chances of the pupils we serve.

Outstanding Teaching started life in Osiris Educational in 2005 as a direct response to the requirements of Ofsted and the feeling that better teaching should lead to enhanced outcomes for all pupils. We felt at the time that whilst learning was ultimately the responsibility of the learner, better teaching had to be the responsibility of the teacher and, as such, all teachers and teacher leaders. Such a direct relationship and the fact that there was already an Ofsted judgement in place to attempt to grade it, offered a strong, recognisable entry point.

Andy Griffith and Mark Burns have been key players in our success and I value and love their work and contribution. Since 2005 they have been in and out of schools, working with teachers at the 'chalk face' to develop this amazing body of work. This is not a personal odyssey of what can be made to work in classrooms, but rather a highly practical guide to what works in classrooms and it is referenced to the very latest Ofsted guidance. This approach is proven through teacher observation, academic research of their work and the feedback of 10,000 teachers who have experienced the Outstanding Teaching training Andy and Mark have delivered.

At the heart of the search for Outstanding Teaching came a number of questions:

- Is it possible for all teachers to teach at an outstanding level?

- Can all schools become Outstanding?

- Do all pupils deserve the right to be taught in Outstanding Schools?

Teacher by teacher, lesson by lesson and pupil by pupil they have begun to work out not only 'yes' to all of the above but how exactly it can be made to happen.

In this, the first of a series of books that demystifies Outstanding Teaching, Andy and Mark unpick pupil engagement as the very bedrock of teacher improvement. Sure, behaviour management is important, but by engaging all pupils in learning, behaviour improves automatically. The reverse is not true. If a teacher, wishing to improve, first focuses on engagement as the number one element, the journey to outstanding begins.

For aspiring teachers, Andy and Mark have made this journey very easy and highly practical. The illustrations in the book and the pages full of activities to use and adapt immediately in your classroom are original, super engaging and timely. They are not a list of top tips from spouters, but are well-researched, progressive and developmental, pedagogical and practical, and great fun for teachers and pupils alike.

I am very proud to put my name to this, the first in the Osiris Outstanding Teaching Series.

Stephen Cox, Founder and MD, Osiris Educational

INTRODUCTION

It's always a good feeling when you bump into an ex-pupil who positively acknowledges you. If they do take the trouble to talk to you we guarantee they won't say something like, 'I've really missed seeing you write up your lesson objectives' or 'I loved the way you differentiated your worksheets'. When an ex-pupil remembers you fondly it will be because you engaged them with their learning and helped them in their lives. We're confident this book will support you to make you and your teaching much more engaging and memorable.

It's a challenging time to be a teacher. Wage freezes, job cuts, league tables, Ofsted, a curriculum overly focused on teaching knowledge and students who present ever more complex forms of resistance to learning. Nevertheless, many teachers still find the job a rewarding one because, unlike so many other professions, we really can make a difference to the lives of others.

It's also a challenging time to be a student. Demonised by the media, molly-coddled by parents and spoon-fed by teachers, they face a world riddled with problems, not least ever more brutal labour markets and increasing global uncertainties.

Yet despite these challenges there are reasons to be cheerful. How teachers are trained is becoming more 'evidence based', squeezing out a lot of the fads and quackery that have blighted our schools in recent years. And despite some surveys to the contrary, we know that teaching is still a profession that many of those on the outside still look up to with admiration and even awe.

Over the last five years, we've been delivering teacher training to thousands of teachers in primary and secondary schools around the country. In particular, we've undertaken extensive work with more than 750 teachers (as of July 2012) in a series of Outstanding Teaching Training Interventions (OTTI). This has provided us with the opportunity and privilege of observing and videoing over 2,000 lessons. In all the many outstanding lessons we've observed, there have always been four common and essential and interdependent ingredients. We refer to these as 'The Big Four'. Increasingly we are referring to them using the acronym FACE.

one **Feedback:** From a teacher perspective, learning needs to be structured to provide opportunities for the teacher to get frequent feedback on the progress of the learners. It's this feedback that informs the direction of the rest of the lesson and all future planning. From a student perspective, as learners move through the education system they need to become increasingly adept at judging the quality of their learning against success criteria and then applying effective strategies to constantly improve the quality of their work.

two **Autonomy**: Lessons need to be structured to reduce teacher talking time, thereby providing the 'oxygen' for learning to take place. Students need space and time to consolidate, extend and deepen their understanding of what they have been taught. To do this students need to have the knowledge, attitudes, skills and habits (KASH) to learn effectively not just from their teacher but also from other sources including their peers.

three **Challenge**: Without challenge there can be no progress; but challenge needs to be differentiated in order to appropriately stretch all students at their different levels of ability.

four **Engagement**: Without engagement nothing else is possible. It provides the glue that binds all the previous elements together. Engagement is characterised by a sense of *flow* – a profound sense of being fully absorbed by whatever it is you're doing. Without this deep kind of engagement it will be very tricky to get students to step up to the challenge of learning. Engagement is essential if they're to become more independent in their learning, develop the confidence and courage to give themselves and each other quality feedback and rise to the challenge of stretching themselves to the limit. For teachers, engagement is the starting point of everything. It's the fertile soil that enables sustainable learning to take root and flourish. Without it the paper aeroplane designers will have a field day! And it's on this element of the Big Four (FACE) – engagement – that we'll focus in this book.

Our Big Four also corresponds closely with another oft-quoted source, Professor John Hattie's seminal work on teacher excellence.[1] The results of his work are very clear: teachers can make the most significant difference to a student's learning, but it's only the truly expert teachers who can do this.

---

1 J. Hattie, *Distinguishing Expert Teachers from Novice and Experienced Teachers. Teachers Make a Difference: What is the Research Evidence?* University of Auckland, Australian Council for Educational Research, October 2003. Available at https://www.det.nsw.edu.au/proflearn/docs/pdf/qt_hattie.pdf (accessed 12 June 2012).

WHAT DO WE MEAN BY ENGAGEMENT?

When we talk about an *engaged* class, we don't just mean the class is compliant and following instructions. Engagement, in the context of this book, refers to the class enjoying and being absorbed in the challenge of their learning and through that engagement making observable progress. We realise that consistently high engagement only really happens when all of the Big Four are in harmony. However, when we work with teachers we only work on one thing at a time. We always start with seeing how good a teacher is at engaging their students and we do this through getting them to explore the 'levels' of their teaching.

WHY WE USE LEVELS

A key element of the way we work with teachers involves the use of graded descriptors and strategies explaining how to 'level up'. Throughout this book we share with you the same set of levels that we use in our training programmes. They will support you to plan, assess and evaluate how good you are at engaging your classes:

Level 1a = Outstanding Secure

Level 1b = Outstanding Unsecure

Level 2a = Good Secure

Level 2b = Good Unsecure

Level 3 = Satisfactory

The levels are calibrated to the latest Ofsted framework which in itself has been highly influenced by John Hattie's conclusions.[2] At each level we illustrate the actions, attitudes and behaviours of both teacher and students and how to move up them.

Many of the teachers we've worked with have told us that they are often confused by Ofsted's criteria for assessing them. Some have said things like: 'I used to know what outstanding looked like but now I'm not so sure.' Others have said that they became even more confused by feedback on their lessons from senior managers. One teacher was told, 'That was a good lesson with some outstanding features, but I can't quite put my finger on

---

2 Ofsted (2012), *The Framework for School Inspection from January 2012*, 30 March 2012. Ref: 090019. Available at http://www.ofsted.gov.uk/resources/framework-for-school-inspection-january-2012 (accessed 12 June 2012).

what would make it outstanding.' How useful is that? Other teachers complain that they have been given contradictory feedback from different members of senior management. This is not a criticism of these teachers, far from it. It is more a reflection on the lack of clarity and guidance from others who are often just as confused as they are.

Ratings, scales or levels do help us is many aspects of our lives. There are 'levels' for restaurants rated by the likes of the famous Michelin Guide. The more stars the restaurant has the better quality dining experience you would expect. Similarly, martial arts move from a white belt up to a black belt and then new levels or dans after that. There are descriptor levels for storms, terrorist alerts and so on. These scales help to inform us and give us information about what to expect.

With all the confusion about Ofsted in mind, we have developed the levels – each one having its own set of descriptors – to provide real clarity and a solid basis for benchmarking. Teachers, like students, require clear success criteria and they need to be aware of the 'gap' between their current level of performance and their potential level. Only when the size of the gap is realised can they apply strategies to try to close it. We've been told by many teachers that working with the levels helps them to fully appreciate where their own teaching practice needs to develop. Therefore the levels provide clear success criteria that are transparent to individual teachers or groups of teachers working together and observers. The levels are designed to support teachers to develop a shared understanding and to apply real quality to the processes of improving teaching and learning.

This book will help you to *live* Assessment for Learning in your teaching. It will help you to judge what level you are currently at for the crucial area of student engagement and how to identify, from the next level descriptor, what you might need to work on to push yourself and your learners on to the next level and beyond.

We know from our own experiences that high-quality education can be transformational – it lifted our families out of poverty. A single teacher can make a massive, positive difference to the life of a young person. Whether you wish to read this book from cover to cover, focus on a particular chapter that attracts you or just dip in and out of certain sections, we're confident you'll find ideas and inspiration to make your teaching more fun, your lessons more engaging and your students more mature, independent and eager to learn. Whether you're an experienced teacher or new to the profession, we hope you enjoy our book.

NB The level descriptors and term 'levelling up' originated in the Osiris Outstanding Teaching Intervention booklet, visit www.osiriseducational.co.uk.

Level 1a

The students demonstrate that they are highly motivated and possess excellent learning dispositions. Students are clearly in FLOW most/all of the time. The students are highly engaged through their own curiosity and enjoyment of the learning/struggle to learn. The teacher has created a student-led lesson (20:80) and acts as activator and challenger. Students are enjoying opportunities to express themselves creatively in a variety of ways and are making rapid progress.

Level 1b

The whole class seem to be highly engaged and are making significant progress in understanding new ideas/concepts through participating in the classroom activities. FLOW is evident for the students as the teacher skilfully creates a student-led lesson (30:70). All discussions are purposeful and there is evidence that students are showing initiative and creativity. Many intrinsic motivators appear to be present.

Level 2a

Nearly all of the students seem to be engaged by the activities and there is clear evidence of enjoyment/understanding why the learning is important. Teacher input (40:60) and there is evidence that students are taking more initiative with their learning. The classroom environment is one of positive relationships and many students are in FLOW because the teacher has set appropriately challenging activities. All students are making good progress.

Level 2b

Most students motivated to participate. There is some evidence that the teacher is building postive relationships with individuals and the class as a whole. Teacher input (50:50) . Some use of intrinsic motivators. The activities used are effective and have good impact on learning. Most students are making good progress.

Engagement (FLOW)

Level 1a + 1b:
Outstanding

Level 2a + 2b:
Good

Level 3:
Satisfactory

Level 3

Nearly all the students are on task, although there may be occasional low level disruption/inertia. Students are engaged in learning but few are getting into FLOW perhaps due to lack of challenge. Less evidence of collaboration, struggle or variety. Teacher input high. Progress is satisfactory.

ICONS THROUGHOUT THE BOOK

Level up: Here we suggest ways to 'level up' your teaching in the area of student engagement. When using this section of the book use the Engaging Learners levels to check your starting point and direction of travel – upwards to 1a.

Reflection point: Here we suggest you reflect on your current practice and how you might change it. Take a little time here to examine whether the suggestions in this section of the book will improve your performance as a teacher.

Eureka moment: Here we offer inspirational ideas and case studies from other teachers. Those teachers have only attained these eureka moments by trying out a new idea. Maybe you could try this too.

Chapter 1

WHY AREN'T THESE KIDS ENGAGED?

WHAT'S IN THIS CHAPTER FOR ME?

- Do you sometimes feel that you're working harder than your learners?

- Have you ever found yourself envying teachers who just have that knack of getting their class doing most of the work?

- Have you ever wished that more of your lessons would flow effortlessly and time would sail by?

- Have you ever wondered how you could create greater enjoyment in learning both for you and your students?

If you answered 'yes' to any of these questions, this chapter is likely to help you achieve greater creativity, balance and satisfaction in your work. Here we'll be exploring the theory behind 'flow'. Flow is a state described by Professor Mihaly Csikszentmihalyi as 'being completely involved in an activity for its own sake. The ego falls away. Time flies. Every action, movement and thought follows inevitably from the previous one, like playing jazz. Your whole being is involved and you're using your skills to the utmost.'[1]

In this chapter we'll explain why flow is crucial to achieving Level 1a engagement in lessons.

---

1 J. Geirland (1996). "Go With The Flow". *Wired* magazine, September, Issue 4.09. (http://www.wired.com/wired/archive/4.09/czik_pr.html).

FLOW: THE *ONLY* THEORY YOU NEED FOR HIGH ENGAGEMENT

For over 30 years, Mihaly Csikszentmihalyi has been the world's leading expert in the field of optimal performance. He first set out studying famous writers, musicians, artists, academics, engineers and Nobel Prize winners trying to discover why and how they attained their high levels of performance.

They described back to him the characteristics of flow – moments when time disappears as you completely lose yourself in the activity you're engaged in. Minutes become hours, hours become days. You become so focused and energised that distractions cannot enter your thoughts. Such activity is highly pleasurable. He refers to these experiences as 'autotelic'.

Csikszentmihalyi widened his search to 'ordinary' people like you and me and has since studied more than 100,000 individuals of all ages, genders, races, backgrounds and occupations. It seems that all his subjects are capable of this state of flow across a vast arena of experiences. For some it comes through their relationships, for others it's in their work, their hobbies or in sporting activity.

Flow occurs when high skill levels meet high challenge as shown in the diagram below. Everybody has had experiences of flow in their lives. A common example that people frequently give is cooking a meal. Concentration is high as they fully utilise their skills to blend the ingredients and coordinate all the different elements of the dish so they are ready simultaneously. The pressure of cooking a meal can easily create flow. However, if the challenge level is lowered to beans on toast, the result may well be boredom as your cooking skills are hardly being extended. At the other end of the scale, if ordinary people were parachuted into top London restaurants and given the responsibility of cooking Michelin-starred cuisine, the likely reaction would be high levels of stress and anxiety.

Even the most challenging teenagers get into flow. Don't believe us? Just listen to them discuss the hours they've spent trying to get to the next level on *Call of Duty* on their PlayStation console or time spent on Facebook.

Csikszentmihalyi's studies of school-age children indicated that there was far too little flow during their school day. Many of the characteristics of the normal school day – such as automated bells, set times for work, externally imposed syllabi and disturbance from peers – constantly interrupt the opportunity for autotelic experiences to develop. Indeed his first book was entitled *Beyond Boredom and Anxiety*.

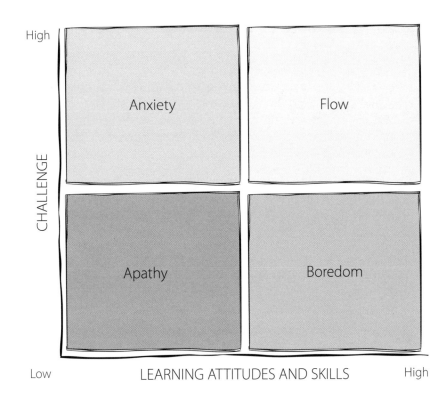

As we can see in the graph above, different combinations of challenge and skill produce a variety of responses. When challenge is low, learning states ranging from boredom to apathy can occur. When skills use is low, learning states can range from apathy to anxiety. Csikszentmihalyi's studies of schools in the United States indicated that students were in a state of apathy for 28% of the time during their lessons. From our own experience of schools, typical activities that produced boredom and apathy in us included traditional dictation, irrelevant worksheets, too much teacher talk, head teacher assemblies and dull comprehension exercises. Getting into a state of flow was a much rarer experience for us. We mostly experienced flow when away from school.

Where flow occurs in the lessons that we observe, students are leading their learning. – they are debating, problem-solving or perhaps working on real-life scenarios. One recent example was a Health and Social Care lesson with a group of really disaffected Year 10 students. The teacher was aiming for the students to learn about some of the factors that prevent agencies from working effectively together on child protection issues. Not a seemingly obvious topic to create flow. However, the teacher based the lesson on an unfolding real-life case history. At the start, the class were unaware that the child would end up dead, killed by her abusive stepmother, while doctors, teachers and social workers failed to intervene.

The students worked in small groups. Each group took on the role of one of the agencies. The teacher skilfully drip-fed information to each group in three stages. After each stage, they were asked what action they would take in the light of the information they held. At the end, the class discovered the child had been killed. This provoked a genuine and emotional reaction. The students then analysed which of the agencies they felt was most culpable for the death of the little girl. The debate was intelligent and purposeful with many students making excellent points. Indeed, the students were working at least two grades higher than their target grades. When the lesson ended, there was a palpable sense of disappointment as the class wanted to go on learning.

How often do your classes get into this state? Once a day? Once a week? Once a term? Once a year? How could you create more flow in your lessons?

In his book, *Visible Learning* (2009), Professor John Hattie examined the statistical evidence about the effects of different teaching methods. His work highlights the crucial importance of both *feedback* and *challenge* to outstanding teaching and learning. He found that expert teachers set tasks that led to deep learning three times as often as experienced non-expert teachers. Deep learning takes place when students are applying, analysing, evaluating and synthesising new learning. Experienced non-expert teachers instead set more tasks that involved surface exploration, mainly content-based learning.

In classrooms where students are insufficiently challenged about their learning and where they don't have opportunities to practise their learning and explain it to others, it will be very difficult for teachers to gain accurate feedback about how their students are progressing. It is essential that as teachers we create sufficient space and opportunities for independent learning in our lessons, so that we can gather real evidence about our students' learning or lack of it. Without this evidence how can we be sure that at the end of the lesson the students really have progressed?

THE SIX FOUNDATIONS OF FLOW

Based upon our 2,000 or so lesson observations, we've found that flow rarely occurs without *all* of the six foundations below being in place:

1   Tasks are appropriately challenging.

2   Teacher input is minimal.

3   Class have the necessary learning skills.

4   Goals are clear and worthwhile.

5   Feedback is immediate.

6   Tasks are intrinsically motivating.

Each element is important. If any are not present the chance of flow occurring significantly recedes. Let's look at these foundations one by one.

TASKS ARE APPROPRIATELY CHALLENGING

What we mean by this is that the each of the ability groups within the class are equally stretched.

We don't mean that every student is working on the same challenging activity. Indeed, there won't be flow where students are totally confused because they are out of their depth or alternatively where students are waiting for others to 'catch up'.

A particularly useful tool for guaranteeing deeper learning and flow in the classroom is Bloom's Taxonomy. This provides a hierarchy of progressively more challenging thinking.

The list in the table below is graded: *Creating* is the most challenging task; *remembering* the least.

Bloom's Revised Taxonomy	
Creating	Putting elements together to form a coherent or functional whole; reorganising elements into a new pattern or structure through generating, planning or producing. This can involve designing, constructing, planning, inventing, devising, programming, filming, animating, blogging, mixing, video-casting and podcasting.
Evaluating	Making judgements based on criteria and standards through checking and critiquing. This can involve hypothesising, critiquing, experimenting, judging, testing, detecting, monitoring and reviewing.
Analysing	Breaking material into constituent parts, determining how the parts relate to one another and to an overall structure or purpose through differentiating, organising and attributing. This can involve comparing, contrasting, organising, deconstructing and attributing.
Applying	Carrying out or using a procedure through executing or implementing. This can involve implementing, carrying out and using.
Understanding	Constructing meaning from oral, written and graphic messages through interpreting, exemplifying, classifying, summarising, inferring, comparing and explaining.
Remembering	Retrieving, recognising and recalling relevant knowledge from long-term memory.

Source: Anderson & Krathwohl (2001), as cited in *Forehand* (2008).

Flow occurs when learners get the chance to move beyond simple remembering and understanding activities. Where lesson objectives are very knowledge or content based there is unlikely to be much flow.

> If you've ever been given feedback that your lesson wasn't challenging or differentiated enough, then there will be lots of ideas in this book on how to address this – see particularly chapters 2 and 3.

TEACHER INPUT IS MINIMAL

What we mean by this is that the teacher has structured the lesson so that there are many opportunities for students to work either individually or collaboratively.

We don't mean that the teacher is sitting at their desk marking or reading a newspaper! They will be circulating the room and gaining feedback on progress.

When working with teachers we talk a lot about creating 30:70 lessons. Many teachers go further and get to 10:90. By 30:70 we mean that only 30% of the lesson is teacher led, while the rest of the time the class leads its own learning. Without this kind of weighting, there simply isn't enough time for learners to get into flow in the lesson. Indeed the only person who is likely to get into flow in a 90:10 lesson (i.e., 90% teacher talking time) is the teacher. One of the most common reactions we get when teachers watch themselves on DVD for the first time is: 'I was shouting at the screen – "Shut up!"' Often they had been aware that they talked a bit too much; but not to the extent that their talking actually hindered learning. They saw that their students had very little opportunity to get into flow for any meaningful period of time. The DVD playback is often a powerful wake-up call to plan much more and talk far less.

> One teacher realised he needed a kind of 'shock therapy' to break his talking habit. He now has a large 'STOP TALKING' sign on the back wall of his classroom. He also uses an egg timer when he gives instructions. His rationale is that if he can't explain the task in less than three minutes then he can't have explained it very well!

The most effective way that we have found to help teachers reduce their talk time is to structure the lesson so that students have periods of time dedicated to independent work so that the teacher can't dominate. If you sense that you're doing too much of the learning for your students then you will get lots of ideas from this book, especially chapters 2 and 6.

CLASS HAVE THE NECESSARY LEARNING SKILLS

What we mean by this is that students have the attitudes, skills and habits to work independently for long periods and cope with the level of challenge their teacher has provided.

We don't mean that the students are simply being well behaved, compliant and have the correct equipment.

It may be that the heyday of Personal, Learning and Thinking skills (PLTs) has passed. Certainly for some teachers they were just another acronym that came and went. However, PLTs did highlight the importance of building the *learning capacity* of classes. Learning capacity means that effective learning of content and knowledge goes hand in hand with students having the necessary skills, attitudes and habits to master them.

Professor Guy Claxton refers to this as 'split screen' teaching.[2] One half of the screen contains the new knowledge or subject-specific skills, that are to be learned; the other holds the learning skills, attitudes and habits that need to be developed alongside.

Many teachers are capable of teaching a Level 1a lesson with some of their classes but not with others. The limiting factor is usually the students' lack of the appropriate attitudes, skills and habits. Claxton refers to this as the students''learning power'. If the students have the necessary learning power they will rise to the occasion if the teacher constructs an effective lesson. If not, they won't. When teachers take time to teach the necessary strategies that develop these areas they will discover that their students can work at considerably higher levels.

---

2 Professor Guy Claxton. Opening Keynote Address, British Educational Research Association Annual Conference, 6 September 2006, Warwick University.

In one Year 5 class in Liverpool the teacher trained her class to celebrate 'stuckness' so that as the year progressed her students became increasingly more independent as problem solvers and more effective as team workers.

In an A level History class, the teacher worked hard from the outset to develop real quality in group discussion and team responsibility so that her students would be able to achieve tasks with much greater independence and self-engagement later in the year.

In both cases these initial efforts by the teachers enabled much more flow to be created in their lessons.

We'll go into in much more detail in this book about how to develop the 'right' learning attitudes, skills and habits of your students, such as taking your class through a focused induction at the start of the school year; see especially Chapter 5.

GOALS ARE CLEAR AND WORTHWHILE

What we mean by this is that students are clear about what they are doing and why they are doing it.

We don't mean that students can just recite the success criteria; they also understand how it fits in with the bigger picture of their improvement in the subject.

The fact is that it's really difficult for anybody to get into flow unless they're clear about what it is they're trying to achieve. So it's crucial that learners fully understand the success criteria that they're working towards. That doesn't just mean that it's been aired and shared, but that there's real and ongoing understanding. Excellent teachers push students to explain what the success criteria are in their own words to make sure they fully understand. Not only do students need to grasp the learning goal for flow to occur; it is also crucial that they know the steps they have to take to achieve the goal. Without this understanding, students' flow is likely to be interrupted. You'll hear them pausing and asking their teacher, 'What do I do next?'

Clarity of direction and purpose is essential for flow. We will focus on how you can give clearer instructions to your students in Chapter 6, and how to help them to increasingly set their own learning goals in Chapter 3.

One particular Year 7 Art lesson springs to mind as an example of confusion about what an effective goal is. The teacher had provided the class with tissues and yellow, blue and red food colouring. The students were not at all clear about what they were aiming for but were initially more than happy to experiment with the resources. But engagement levels soon dropped as the students' interest waned. After the teacher had had a chance to reflect on the lesson and why engagement was low, he had a 'eureka' moment. They didn't have any idea what the desired outcome would look like. Instead they experimented with the tissues and food colouring and only succeeded in making quite a mess.

When the teacher repeated the lesson with a similar class, he showed them examples of the desired outcome. These were tissues that showed the full range of secondary and tertiary colours. Subsequently the engagement of the class was far higher. Students were absolutely clear on what they were aiming for. In particular they relished the challenge of puzzling out which colours needed to be combined to create the tertiary colours.

FEEDBACK IS IMMEDIATE

What we mean by this is that students can give feedback and receive it from their peers. They are able to self-assess accurately and where necessary take corrective action.

We don't mean that the teacher is necessarily the source of feedback at all times, rushing around the room answering the perennial 'Is this right, Miss?' Indeed at Level 1a/b, students will be able to self-assess and peer-assess accurately and act on the feedback given independently of their teacher.

Where flow occurs in lessons, students can get regular and accurate feedback about their progress. 'Am I doing this right?' or 'Is this the best way to complete this task?' will be two essential questions students need to be asking, but this can present an enormous challenge to the teacher. How do you provide this level of detailed, prompt feedback to 30 students at once?

There is another way. Many teachers we have worked with have tried to increase student ownership of giving and receiving feedback. They have worked hard to train their students to assess their own work accurately. They've also developed the attitudes and skills of their students so that they can give feedback and receive it from their peers. As a result, they are no longer dependent on feedback from their teacher. As a consequence, flow is much more common.

Getting students to take more responsibility for their own feedback can be achieved through creating the right classroom environment. We particularly explore how to do this in chapters 4 and 5.

To what extent do your classes depend upon you for improvement guidance and goal setting?

Could your students take more ownership of giving and acting on feedback?

Have you got the balance right?

TASKS ARE INTRINSICALLY MOTIVATING

What we mean by this is that students are doing the task not because they have to but rather because they are keen to. They are enthusiastic to take part and contribute because they find what they are doing to be personally enjoyable.

We don't mean that students are being coerced or bribed to learn.

A great example of this occurred in a Year 11 Maths lesson where a group of low ability, disaffected girls were in flow. The girls, working in pairs, had to decide how they were going to spend their budget on a Valentine's Day meal and gift. The room had been arranged with menus and flowers. At one point the teacher went to ask one pair how they were getting on. The response? 'Leave us alone, Miss, you're distracting us from our learning!' Using the intrinsic motivational triggers of *relevance* and *fantasy* the teacher created a highly engaging lesson. Her most difficult class had been transformed into Maths addicts!

Motivating students can be many teachers' number one problem. We particularly explore how to do this in chapters 3 and 4.

FAQS

Is there a lower age limit for learners getting into flow?

Not that we've seen and we've observed nursery up to Year 13. Go into an outstanding Early Years setting and there's tons of flow on show!

But surely I'll need time to teach the new information?

Yes, there will be certain lessons when teachers need to talk more. However, every lesson needs time and space when learners work to demonstrate what they have learned. This is the time when flow is crucial.

Is it only practical subjects where flow is relevant?

No, we've seen examples of flow in lessons covering every subject on the curriculum.

Is creating more flow in lessons one of the secrets to feeling less knackered at the end of term?

Flow won't stop the ageing process but we reckon getting your learners regularly into flow not only takes the pressure off you, but also helps you enjoy your teaching a lot more.

Great! When can I start?

Next time you're in your classroom.

IN A NUTSHELL

Outstanding lessons contain lots of flow. Flow is a state where learners work independently, are deep in concentration and totally immersed in their learning. Students are doing what they want to do, not what they feel they are being made to do. To create flow in lessons the following conditions are essential: tasks are appropriately challenging and intrinsically motivating; teacher input is minimal; the class have the necessary learning skills; goals are clear and worthwhile; and feedback is immediate

FOR MORE INFORMATION ...

Watch Csikszentmihalyi's lecture on Ted.com:

http://www.ted.com/talks/mihaly_csikszentmihalyi_on_flow.html.

Or read the book:

Mihaly Csikszentmihalyi, *Flow: The Psychology of Optimal Experience* (New York: Simon & Schuster, 1990).

Chapter 2

THAT WAS GREAT – MY BRAIN HURT

WHAT'S IN THIS CHAPTER FOR ME?

- Have you ever wished you had access to a bank of creative and effective teaching ideas for getting your students into flow?

- Have you ever wanted access to practical and workable activities that will engage and challenge learners and encourage them to develop excellent learning habits and skills?

- Have you ever wondered how you might increase progress and enjoyment both for your students and yourself?

If you're looking for practical ways to reduce the ratio of teacher to student talk time then this chapter offers you a raft of tried and tested ideas that encourage higher levels of challenge and accelerate student progress. This chapter takes the theory of the previous chapter and translates it into action.

Most teachers we know would love to have that 'redundant' feeling more often in their lessons. How would it be for you if your class were able to work independently, totally absorbed in their work for 20 minutes or more?

Our work with teachers has focused on helping them create more moments like these, where students are immersed in their learning and are working much harder than their teachers.

Picture the scene: windy day, Portakabin classroom, decaying school buildings, last lesson on a Friday afternoon. And one more thing, in those days the school was still in special measures. The odds seemed to be stacked against the teacher before we'd started. However, what unfolded that day was utterly inspirational and we sat open mouthed whilst filming what was the best English lesson we'd ever seen. The Year 11 class were totally in flow analysing the connections between themes and characters from Steinbeck's *Of Mice and Men*. All the students were busily engaged, referring to their notes, the text and collaborating in small groups. (We'll look at exactly how the teacher did this later in the chapter.) Halfway through the lesson she came over to us and said, 'I've got a big problem!' We gave her puzzled expressions, 'But it's going brilliantly!' 'I know,' she replied, 'but I need to move on and they won't want to stop!'

WHAT'S THE THINKING BEHIND THIS CHAPTER?

Look again at the Level 1a descriptor below. To reach Level 1a requires lessons to be student led. We use the ratio 20:80 in terms of teacher talk to student talk. This can only happen where teachers provide challenges for learners that get them working at high levels on Bloom's Taxonomy for long periods. Unless you provide activities that offer appropriate complexity, students will not get into flow and will become disengaged.

Level 1a: The students demonstrate that they are highly motivated and possess excellent learning dispositions. Students are clearly in FLOW most/all of the time. The students are highly engaged through their own curiosity and enjoyment of the learning/struggle to learn. The teacher has created a student-led lesson (20:80) and acts as activator and challenger. Students are enjoying opportunities to express themselves creatively in a variety of ways and are making rapid progress.

As we stated in Chapter 1, the more tools a teacher has for creating flow in lessons, the easier it is to engage and challenge learners across all the different topics that are taught in schools. If we don't have access to these tools or don't use them, it will be a major barrier to transforming the ratio of teacher talk to student talk. In this chapter we'll explore some of the activities that can work brilliantly in creating flow in lessons; activities we've seen used with great success all around the country.

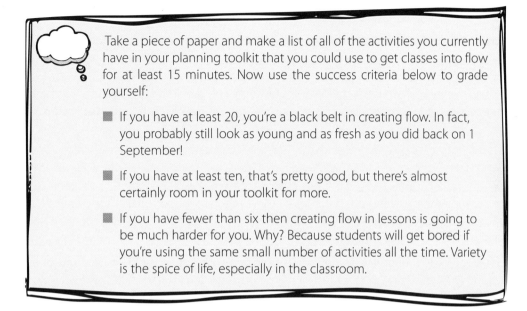

Take a piece of paper and make a list of all of the activities you currently have in your planning toolkit that you could use to get classes into flow for at least 15 minutes. Now use the success criteria below to grade yourself:

- If you have at least 20, you're a black belt in creating flow. In fact, you probably still look as young and as fresh as you did back on 1 September!

- If you have at least ten, that's pretty good, but there's almost certainly room in your toolkit for more.

- If you have fewer than six then creating flow in lessons is going to be much harder for you. Why? Because students will get bored if you're using the same small number of activities all the time. Variety is the spice of life, especially in the classroom.

WHAT DO WE MEAN BY DIFFERENTIATION?

It is absolutely vital that the challenge level is appropriate for all students. Ignore differentiation and you will identify groups of learners who are not in flow because the challenge level is too low or too high. Differentiation is fundamental to ensuring all students make the 'rapid and sustained progress' that Ofsted characterise as 'outstanding'. In this chapter we are referring to differentiation by task and not by outcome.

Three of the most effective activities for building flow into lessons are Learning Grids, Trump Cards and Tarsia. We've chosen these because of their adaptability. They provide both *complexity* and *challenge* for learners and they naturally encourage the emergence of intrinsic motivation. We'll indicate the stages of Bloom's Taxonomy that each activity requires the learners to work at and the types of skills each particular activity develops.

LEARNING GRIDS

We confess to being unashamed addicts of Learning Grids. If we had to pick the one single activity that can get a class into flow even when it's snowing and blowing a force 10 gale outside, we reckon this is the one! We also love it because of its adaptability. The first time we encountered Learning Grids was on a course run by Stephen Bowkett, a really creative English teacher and story writer. If you teach English we highly recommend his books.

Learning Grids are activities for students working in pairs. Learning in pairs provides opportunities for collaborative learning, enabling students to discuss their learning and to peer-teach each other. When groups are larger there's always a greater risk of some students dominating while others sit back. There are also opportunities for one pair of students to work with another pair during or at the end of an activity to compare and contrast their learning.

In terms of equipment, the students will need a die each. We use foam dice which are delightfully silent – much more restful than the horrendous clatter of 30 traditional dice rattling around on students' desk tops. Students use the dice to determine which cell in the grid they will use. Our first example of a Learning Grid is one that could be used to practise the skill of a specific writing genre. Look for ways you could adapt it to your own topics and subject area.

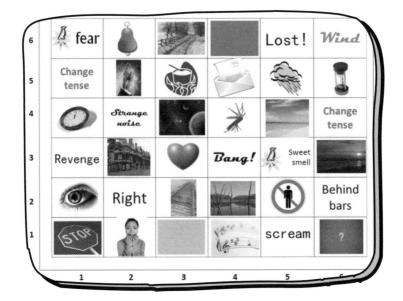

The first step is to ask each pair to roll one of their dice. This score determines the genre of their story, for example, (1) gothic horror, (2) western, (3) romance, (4) adventure, (5) crime and (6) fantasy. With the genre established, the story writing can begin. The first student rolls the die. This will determine the number on the horizontal axis. Let's say he rolls a 3. His partner now rolls the second die which determines the number on the vertical axis. Let's say she rolls another 3. The word or image located in this cell, in this case a heart, is now used by the pair to write the first sentence in their story. If their genre is crime it might start:

The detective's heart missed a beat as he slipped into the dimly lit quayside warehouse.

Then they roll their dice again; let's say they score 2 and 5. They move to this new cell and continue their story with another sentence. In this case, the hand with fingers crossed:

He couldn't believe his luck, there was his old foe.

And so on. Typically we would give students 15 minutes working together to construct their stories. We also give them a 'two minutes to go' warning so that they can craft a suitable ending. Afterwards we give students the opportunity to share their stories and peer-assess. This might involve identifying particular techniques that work well within each genre and then allowing pairs time to redraft sections that could be improved. We might also encourage a debate about how language and language patterns differ from one genre to another. Suitable homework might be that students create a genre-specific grid of their choice that incorporates a mix of suitable words and images.

But, you might ask, why go to the trouble of using this activity? Does it really work? It works because it incorporates many of the motivational triggers that naturally engage us as human beings. First, there is the randomness of the dice determining how the story is going to develop. This provokes *curiosity*. Next, students are faced with a *challenge* as they are forced to think about how they will incorporate the information from the grid into their story. In addition, the students have to make real *choices* and use their *imagination* as step by step they create the story themselves. In fact, even if two different pairs chose the same genre and roll the dice with exactly the same numbers, they would still write two completely different stories. At the core of this activity is a creative and challenging structure which supports the students to fully engage with their learning and get into deep states of flow.

AT WHICH LEVELS OF BLOOM'S TAXONOMY ARE THEY WORKING?

This activity naturally pushes learners up the levels of Bloom's Taxonomy. This is because it's not an activity based solely on knowledge. It requires students to apply their knowledge about genres to different contexts, to analyse and evaluate suitable language and synthesise it in the creation of new stories. Do the students understand genre-specific writing? Well, they absolutely must do so if they can create a story of their own which is true to the genre.

> One student from a school on Merseyside put her finger on it when she said the best lessons for her were those she hadn't been able to 'Google'. In other words, these were lessons that went above and beyond mere facts and knowledge. Her teachers were skilfully taking her to places where facts and information were contextualised in a far richer and deeper learning.

PRACTISING A SKILL

Students will often need to repetitively practise a skill in lessons in order to achieve mastery. Handled unimaginatively this can be a dull process. However, by embedding these tasks and skills in a Learning Grid, the amount of repetition is disguised. Students get the learning and enjoy the process. In his book *Outliers* (2008), Malcolm Gladwell suggests that as much as 10,000 hours of practice are necessary to achieve a world-class level of performance. Whether this number is accurate or not, the point is that repetition is essential for the mastery of most skills. The more we can make it an engaging rather than a boring practice, the better for us and our students.

Here are three examples:

SIMPLIFYING ALGEBRA

6	2x	(x+1)	(x + 6)	10	6x	(x+30)
5	(x+50)	8	(x-10)	x⁴	(x-50)	x³
4	(x+8)	4x	-2x	(x-15)	(x-4)	3x
3	(x+4)	6	(x+25)	(x-8)	(x-1)	-x
2	x	(x+5)	(x-2)	25	(x-7)	(x-30)
1	(x+20)	(x-5)	10x	2x²	5	2x⁵
	1	2	3	4	5	6

Source: Rebecca Richardson

How to use: This grid is from a Maths lesson where the teacher wanted the students to practise a particular skill: simplifying algebraic expressions by removing brackets. In pairs, the students used dice to identify two cells and then worked together to expand and simplify the expression. This done, they rolled the dice again and moved on.

After completing: After 10 minutes, the teacher asked each pair to swap their answers with another pair. They then had to identify which two cells had been used to lead to each of the answers. This worked a treat: students were collaborating at each stage. All that could be heard was a fantastic hum of productive discussion throughout. The teacher's plenary focused on the methods used and unpicked where mistakes had been made and why.

DESCRIPTIVE ENGLISH

In an English lesson, students were given the Learning Grid below and in pairs asked to select a cell using the dice. The aim of the activity was for the class to practise using a range of descriptive writing techniques. The images in the grid were all linked to the theme of the seaside.

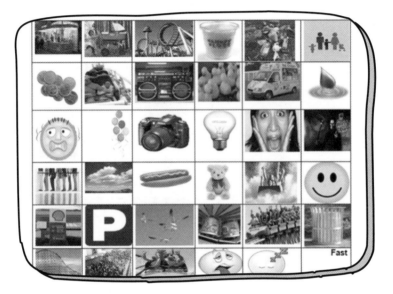

Source: Louise Kilroe

How to use: The students used the image in the cell as inspiration to write a descriptive sentence using one or more descriptive writing techniques. They then rolled the dice again, identified a new cell and wrote another descriptive sentence. They continued this for around 10 minutes while the teacher stood dumbfounded at the work rate of a group that she had previously experienced as reluctant, low-ability learners.

After completing: Reflecting on learning is crucial and the teacher provided time for the class to peer-assess. Each pair of students swapped their list of sentences with another pair. They were then given 5 minutes to decide which were the three best sentences and to identify which were the techniques that had made them so effective, such as simile or metaphor.

APPLYING SKILLS IN ART

This third example of practising skills using a Learning Grid comes from an Art class.

	1	2	3	4	5	6
1	Tone using Pencil	Pen (cross hatching)	Combine two medias	Felt pen	Oil pastel	Paint
2	Paint	Tone Pencil	Pen (cross hatching)	Combine Three Medias	Chalk Pastel	Oil pastel
3	Oil pastel	Paint	Tone Pencil	Pen (cross hatching)	Free Choice	Pencil crayon
4	Felt pen	Oil pastel	Paint	Tone Pencil	Pen (cross hatching)	Combine two medias
5	Chalk Pastel	Chalk Pastel	Oil pastel	Paint	Tone Pencil	Pen (cross hatching)
6	Pen (cross hatching)	Pencil Crayon	Mixed media	Oil pastel	Paint	Tone

Source: Maxine Carrick

How to use: The teacher wanted her class to practise using different media and combining them in creative ways. She gave her class a selection of different outline drawings to choose from. The students then worked in pairs, rolling dice to select a cell such as 2.2, the tone pencil. They then decided where to apply this technique on their outline drawing. The class were completely in flow for the entire lesson. The teacher noted how using the grid had significantly improved not only the students' engagement and concentration, but also the speed at which they worked and the amount of progress they were making. What raised a smile as one of us observed the lesson was the desperation of one pair of boys to land on the 'free choice' cell!

After completing: The students subsequently peer-assessed their work. They reflected on which techniques had worked particularly well and why.

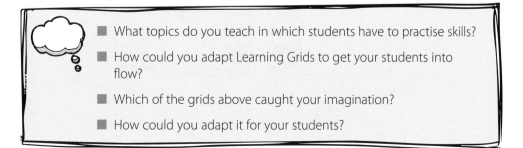

- What topics do you teach in which students have to practise skills?
- How could you adapt Learning Grids to get your students into flow?
- Which of the grids above caught your imagination?
- How could you adapt it for your students?

DIFFERENTIATING LEARNING GRIDS

As we pointed out in Chapter 1, providing exactly the same activity for all the students in your class is unlikely to get them into flow because they will each have different levels of skill. Differentiation can be easily achieved with Learning Grids by changing a small number of cells in the grid to make them more or less challenging. At first glance the activity looks the same, but it isn't.

Some teachers encourage their students to self-select the level of challenge at which they want to work. These levels might be labelled gold, silver or bronze. For the Maths Learning Grid above, the teacher removed all the numbers and replaced them with purely algebraic expressions for the two most able students. This got them really challenged for the first time in weeks.

MAKING LINKS

Back to that great English lesson on Steinbeck's *Of Mice and Men* at the start of the chapter. The class were using the grid below at a later stage of the lesson:

Source: Katie Lorimer

This grid had a different purpose to the previous one. Working in pairs and using dice, students had to select two cells and then make links between them. The random selection of two cells can be used in many different contexts, such as challenging students to compare and contrast different concepts or identifying cause and effect relationships between things. Learning Grids are suitable for adaptation all the way up to KS5 lessons.

Here's another example of using Learning Grids to make links from an RE lesson. Students rolled their dice and then worked together to write a definition and short explanation of the topic contained in the cell. Then the teacher challenged them to roll the dice twice, select two cells and make links between them. The head teacher, who happened to be watching, said it was the best RE lesson she'd ever seen!

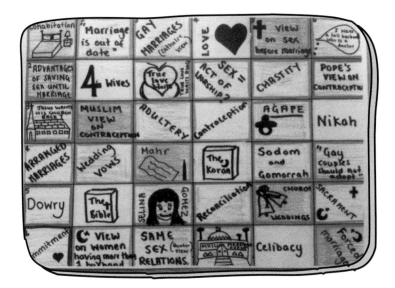

Source: Kerry Burns

EXAM PREPARATION

The British education system, particularly at secondary level, has an addiction to exams. So much so that teachers in many KS4 and KS5 classrooms find themselves revising for an impending exam almost constantly. It can be a real challenge to engage students in revision lessons and create and maintain that vital sense of flow.

Two Science teachers we've worked with use creative adaptations of Learning Grids to keep their students engaged and in flow. Both of them use the 'making links' approach outlined above but also incorporate a number of '?' cells. When students land on a question mark they have to collaborate to answer a past exam paper question.

The example below is from a KS3 Science class who were studying Health and Well-being. The students were in flow for more than 20 minutes in what was an outstanding lesson. The questions used were from GCSE past papers so the challenge level was high for everyone.

Source: Joanna Robertson

This next example comes from a KS4 Chemistry revision lesson and included a further creative twist. This lesson was the last before this class of able students sat their GCSE paper. They were given three grids on different topics. This was sensible as there is little point in revising a topic you already know. Their teacher included a number of '?' cells, as in the previous example, which required students to answer an exam question. However, she also included a number of examiner cells on the grid. If students landed on one of these, they had to mark one of the written answers that had been completed by another pair.

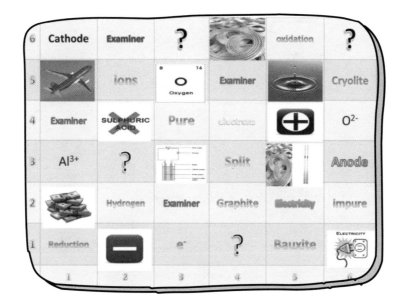

Source: Ruth Howarth

This challenged students to do several things: (1) refine their understanding of exam techniques; (2) feel more confident about the relevant success criteria; and (3) identify areas of the syllabus where they needed to focus their remaining revision time.

HOMEWORK TIP

Get your students to create Learning Grids for their homework. You can use these with other classes and it will save you time and energy – you don't have to create all the resources yourself! It will provide you with a resource bank for the next time you teach the topic. In addition, for many students this will be a more engaging and valuable piece of homework. It is a great way for students to demonstrate their understanding of a topic.

A Year 13 student really challenged his History classmates with this Elizabethan foreign policy grid. It had the effect of getting them and his teacher, into flow.

Marriage negotiations between Elizabeth and the Duke of Anjou?	Assassination of William of Orange?	1564	1585	1603	Portuguese Expedition?
1589	Treaty of Joinville between Philip II and the French Catholic League?	Treaty of Berwick?	Treaty of Troyes?	1584	Treaty of Edinburgh?
1594	1599	Tyrone Rebellion?	1562	1572	Defeat of the Spanish Armada?
Assassination of the Earl of Moray?	Treaty of Cateau Cambresis?	1584	Outbreak of Civil war in France?	Capture of the Treasure ship Madre de Dios?	Year treaty of Nonsuch was created?
Peace negotiations between Mountjoy and Tyrone?	1579	1594	1588	1560	1584
1559	Capture of Cadiz?	Essex's Arrival in Ireland?	1570	St Bartholomew Massacre?	1596

Source: Carmel Bones

The rules were as follows: students rolled dice in the way described earlier to identify a cell. If the cell contained an event, they had to identify the date of the event and its impact on the associated country. The countries were coded by colour: blue for Scotland, green for Ireland, yellow for Spain and Portugal, red for France and orange for the Netherlands. The student built ambiguity into the activity as there are a range of possible implications for each country.

However, if students landed on a purple cell, they had to explain aspects of the relationships between Elizabethan England and the other foreign powers for that year. There was an element of competition too. The students worked in pairs and were playing against each other.

A nominated textbook was the arbiter of any disputes. When students successfully answered the questions raised by a cell to everyone's satisfaction, they shaded it in. The winning pair was the first to shade in the complete grid.

Other adaptations of Learning Grids are to practise skills in classification and analysis. For example, students have to classify the contents of a cell and justify their thinking. This can be made more complex by building in ambiguity so that students have to declare any assumptions they have made in reaching their decision. Perhaps you want your students to analyse the similarities and differences at various stages in a sequence or process, such as the water cycle or the rock cycle. Each time they land on a cell, students are challenged to explain where this particular stage fits in the process and why.

GENERATING IDEAS

In some subjects, such as Technology or Business Studies, students need to analyse how customer needs can impact on the product or service provided. The cells in a Learning Grid might contain information about the age or gender of the consumer, their income, details about their lifestyle and so on. The students roll the dice and select three different cells. They then have to design their product and/or its marketing to suit the different needs and values of these three customer groups. One great advantage of this kind of activity is that the dice ensure random selection. When the students present their redesigned products to the rest of the class, the audience can pay attention at multiple levels. For example, they can listen to, praise and critique the content and the process.

LEARNING GRIDS AND CONCEPT MAPPING

Another excellent tool to get students to synthesise their understanding of a topic is concept mapping. A concept map is a diagram showing the relationships that exist between concepts. It's a graphical tool for organising and representing knowledge.

Here is an example of a Learning Grid from a Year 13 Business Studies lesson.

Unemployment	Enlargement of EU	Social responsibility	Exchange rates	Increased income tax rates	Organic growth
Stakeholders	Takeovers	Technological change	Income elasticity of demand	Differentiation	Off-shoring
Organisational size	Employee participation	Raised interest rates	Economies of scale	Business cycle	ROCE
Short-termism	Gearing	Union density	UK minimum wage	Globalisation	Product development
Motivation	Inflation	Liquidity	Pricing strategy	Recruitment	Tighter EU health and safety legislation
Price of oil	Price elasticity of demand	Performance of competitors	Labour productivity	GDP	Market competitiveness

Students worked in pairs and rolled the dice to select a cell. They copied the concept from the cell onto a piece of A3 paper and then added a definition. They then selected another cell by rolling the dice and repeated the procedure. Now the pair had to work together to find a link between the two concepts. They then added another concept in the same way, building their concept map step by step.

This activity is useful in several ways.

■ It helps students identify areas of confusion, especially if they lack clarity about any of the key concepts.

■ It helps them to realise how different concepts can align. For example, a company might adopt socially responsible policies in order to create a unique selling point for their products.

■ Another added bonus is that this kind of work really encourages creativity and flexibility in students' thinking.

■ How could you use Learning Grids to deepen the engagement of students in the classes you teach?

■ What topics will you be teaching in the next few weeks where Learning Grids could provide real opportunities to increase student engagement and flow?

TRUMP CARDS

Anyone of a certain vintage will remember the craze for Top Trumps in the 1970s. Now they're having something of a renaissance. For those unfamiliar with Top Trumps, it's a trading card game. Each pack of cards is based on a theme, such as cars, aircraft, dinosaurs or characters from popular films or television series. Each card in the pack shows a list of data about the item. For example, in a pack based on cars each card might show a different model, with various information and stats about its engine size, weight, length and top speed. If the theme concerns a TV series or film, the cards include characters and their qualities such as strength, bravery, fashion-sense and looks.

The game is played as follows. All of the cards are dealt out as equally as possible among the players. Each player then turns over their top card without showing it to their rivals. Player 1 in the group chooses a category that she thinks is likely to outscore her rivals. For example, if they are playing with a pack based on cars, she might call out the top speed of the car on her card. The other players then call out the top speed from their own card. Whoever has the highest top speed wins and takes the other players' card. The game continues with the winner then choosing a category from their next card. The person who manages to get all of the cards from their rivals is the winner.

This is a game of analysis and evaluation. Players need to assess all of the data on their card and decide which one is strongest and therefore most likely to outscore their rivals. We've seen this Trump Cards idea adapted in many different ways across many different subjects, particularly where learners need to analyse, compare, contrast and rank information and ideas.

We believe these activities work best and more learning is involved, when students research and create the cards themselves. A Science teacher recently said to us, 'Oh yes, we use these Trump Card games already. We bought a class set which feature elements from the periodic table. We get the students to play the game.' However, we believe it's more important for students to research and make the cards than for them to play the game – this is where the real learning takes place.

One primary teacher created Roald Dahl card templates and invited her students, working in small groups, to create cards for the different characters. They discussed and agreed scores for the different qualities of each character, justifying their score with evidence from the texts. The template below shows how this was done. This work really got the class into flow and the quality of debate was hugely impressive as they debated whether James (he of the Giant Peach) was brainier than the BFG.

Some English teachers we've worked with have challenged their classes to create a series of Trump Cards for a central character in a play or novel. The cards are used for each scene or chapter so that the students can more rigorously analyse how aspects of the character change over time. A good example would be the development of Romeo's character in Shakespeare's *Romeo and Juliet*. The reverse side of the card can provide space for quotes and page references which would be used to justify the scores given.

The challenge of attributing a numeric score to a particular characteristic or quality of a person, feature or object can create fantastic discussion and has the potential for rich questioning. This worked brilliantly in an A level PE lesson where students had to agree on the five key characteristics necessary to be a Premier League football referee. They then created cards for different referees, using data and examples from recent matches to assess their performance across the five characteristics. This activity really helped the students to analyse and understand the complex skill-set that referees require to operate at this level.

The following example is from a Physics lesson. Students had to compile Trump Cards with four pieces of information for several different cars. The information required was:

1   Acceleration (m/s2)

2   Time taken to reach 96 km/h (in seconds)

3   Time taken to reach top speed (in seconds)

4   Distance covered reaching top speed (in metres)

Source: Rebecca Graham

The activity helped the teacher assess the students' understanding of speed/time graphs and the associated formulae.

Differentiation

The task of completing Trump Cards can easily be differentiated by providing more/less evidence to help/confuse students whilst they are compiling the cards.

For many more ideas of how to adapt Trump Cards for other subjects we suggest visiting http://www.tes.co.uk/teaching-resources/ and search for 'top trumps'.

TRUMP CARDS IN ASSESSMENT FOR LEARNING

Most teachers we work with would love to do one or more of the following:

- Build their students' skills in peer- and self-assessment.

- Reduce the amount of preparation they do.

- Spend less time correcting the same mistakes in homework.

We've seen teachers use Trump Cards to help address all these issues. In a Technology lesson, the teacher got the class to decide on the criteria by which to assess coursework examples from a previous year group (see example below). This provoked a rich 10-minute discussion amongst the class as there had to be exactly six criteria for the card. Having agreed on the criteria, the students worked in pairs and assessed one of the pieces of coursework that were distributed around the room.

The students had to identify the strengths in the coursework as well as areas that needed improvement. Following this activity, the teacher asked the students to self-assess their own coursework. He was really impressed by their ability to accurately identify the strengths and weaknesses apparent in their own work. He attributed this to the activity they'd done and in particular the use of the cards in helping them to determine the key criteria.

Source: Dave Jones

We've seen other teachers develop this idea even further so that the students use Trump Cards to help them assess essays or pieces of coursework. This activity really helps the students to deepen their understanding about what they need to do with their essays and coursework to achieve higher grades.

In one example, students working in pairs were given three exemplar essays or pieces of coursework and a Trump Card for each. On each Trump Card were written the various assessment criteria (e.g., example, knowledge, application, analysis, evaluation). The pairs now had to identify whether there was any evidence for the presence of each category and, if so, the score they would give it. By providing students with three essays of differing quality, they used a variety of complex learning skills to improve their understanding of how grades are assessed.

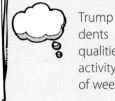

Trump Cards activities are especially well suited to topics where students need to compare, contrast and rank ideas, theories, criteria, qualities, characters and people. How could you adapt a Trump Cards activity and challenge one of your classes with it during the next couple of weeks?

TARSIA

Tarsia is a nifty piece of free software which is usually lurking on school computer networks without many people other than the Maths department knowing about it. Tarsia is open source software and you can download it at http://www.mmlsoft.com/.

Once installed, the software is really easy to use and enables complex jigsaw style puzzles to be created in less than 10 minutes. After you have input your information the software will create a puzzle automatically for you. You then print it and cut it and it's ready to use. Simple!

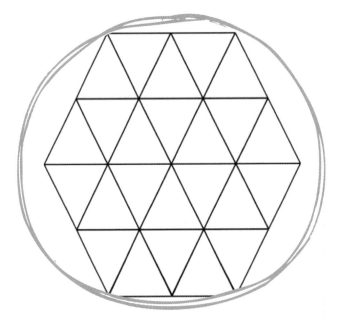

To solve the puzzle, students have to match up the sides of the triangles so that they complement or correspond with each other in some way. Given that a pair of students might be working for more than 25 minutes solving one of these puzzles, Tarsia offers you just the sort of sustainable planning that ensures you don't burn out within two weeks of the start of term!

These puzzles require minimal preparation. You can even get the students to cut out the triangles for you. Working in pairs, it should take them just a few minutes. There are a range of shapes to choose from when designing the puzzle. For secondary students we'd recommend the standard hexagonal shape.

Puzzles are particularly useful when you want to assess your students' comprehension of key concepts or get them to apply their understanding of a topic. We've seen them work brilliantly in a wide range of subjects including Maths, Science, Geography, History, English, PE, Business Studies and language lessons from KS2 through to KS5.

Here is an example from a KS4 Chemistry lesson on electrolysis where students have to match key words to definitions and examples.

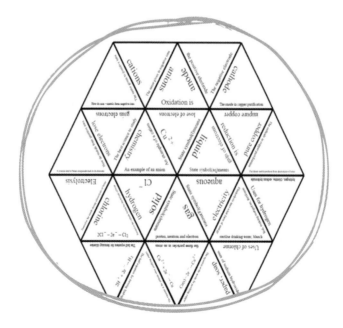

Source: Nicola Eyres

 Avoid helping the students directly and let them engage with the struggle. Encourage them to use their notes or textbooks. Some teachers we have worked with give three question tokens to each pair. If the students get really stuck, the teacher will answer a question – but it costs them a question token! Great psychology!

Tarsia works well because students are engaged by the challenge it presents and the feeling of elation when they complete it. It also encourages student–student questions and independence from the teacher, while the complexity of the puzzle really tests the learning of students.

Differentiation for Tarsia

Tarsia puzzles can be made more challenging very easily. To introduce differentiation you can:

- Build in more ambiguity (e.g., in an English lesson by using visual metaphors for characters in a story or quotes from the text).
- Include more than one possible correct answer.
- Remove several triangles and ask students to identify possible solutions.
- Challenge early finishers to create an outer ring for another group.
- Provide a simpler shape – shapes with irregular pieces are easier to place.
- Include images instead of descriptions.

How about this for differentiation! Chemistry teacher Judith Skimming used the Tarsia below with her A2 Chemistry students. They were allowed to use their notes and collaborate to find the solution. All the students were highly engaged by the puzzle and it took the first group 17 minutes to successfully solve it.

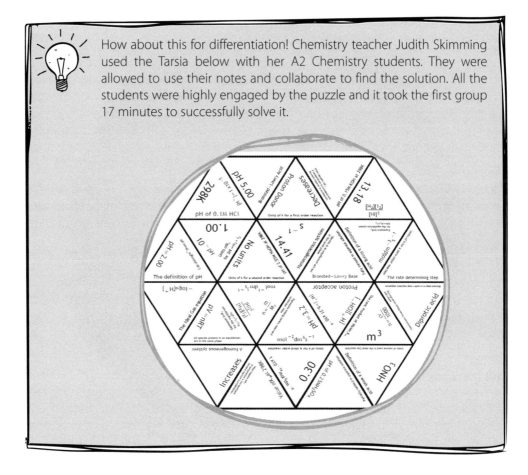

Quite a few teachers we have worked with have taken the logical next step and got their students to create these puzzles for homework. This is a useful learning or revision activity for your students and increases your bank of resources. All you need is to teach them how to use the software. They'll probably understand it quicker than you did!

Where in your teaching could you try out a Tarsia puzzle during the next couple of weeks?

One final piece of advice. We recommend you print off a 'master copy' of the solution to each puzzle so that if students get completely lost you can quickly provide them with advice.

We cannot stress enough that it's always crucially important to *start with the end in mind* when planning for 'outstanding'. Decide first what knowledge, skills or understanding you want the class to learn or demonstrate. Then identify what the students have to say, do or demonstrate that would offer evidence that they have mastered this knowledge, under-standing or skill-set. Finally and only then, can you select the most suitable activity. It will be the one that most elegantly supports your students to achieve the lesson's goals.

We have witnessed all the activities in this chapter working brilliantly in hundreds of class-rooms to create engagement, flow and fast enjoyable learning. And they always work best when the teachers have done their preparation *with the end in mind*. They haven't worked nearly so well when teachers have chosen the activity simply because it's engaging. In these lessons, where the planning has not been sufficiently rigorous, the students have not been able to provide evidence that the success criteria have been met.

FAQS

Will these tools guarantee flow in my lesson?

Guarantees and classes of schoolchildren do not necessarily go hand in hand! We can confidently state that we have seen these tools being used successfully in a wide range of contexts: schools in special measures, schools in inner cities as well as those in more leafy surroundings and with low and high ability students. When they have been less effective it has usually been due to other factors, such as lack of clear instructions or because the learners lacked the capacity to work independently for long periods. However, what we have consistently found is that when used well these activities can have a marked impact on the engagement level of students and their learning.

Won't they get bored with Tarsia after a while?

Yes, familiarity can breed contempt. Mix up these activities with others in the book and ones you already know and have found effective. Look for a wider range of student-led activities that enable you to talk less and get them to work harder.

Won't this require more planning?

Yes, it may do in the short term. But there are many benefits in the longer term and ways to ease the amount of work you have to do. Get together with other teachers in your own and other departments and plan these activities collaboratively. Sharing your teaching resources in an activity pool can really ease the workload. Many teachers also set their students the task of creating resources as homework. This helps you and also supports the learning of the students. Many teachers we work with are prepared to go the extra mile because they see the benefit for themselves and their students in terms of higher levels of engagement, more flow and deeper learning. There is also the additional fact that they enjoy being a teacher more as a result.

I've got so much content to get through before the exam, I'm not sure there's time for more student-led learning ...

Think about using student-led learning particularly in those sections of the lesson where it's important that students provide you with evidence that enables you to accurately assess their learning. Getting the learning right in the lesson means less time spent correcting homework. It will also give you more accurate information when planning for later lessons. All the international studies and research into what makes expert teachers 'outstanding' show that quality feedback to the teacher about what has or has not been learnt is absolutely crucial.

IN A NUTSHELL

The biggest obstacle to change for many of the teachers we work with is not an unwillingness to encourage more student-led learning; it is that they are unsure *how* to create it. Very often this is because they lack the tools and strategies to do this. Generally speaking, if a teacher is in the habit of talking too much, the chances are that they don't have a very large toolkit of activities to create flow. The activities in this chapter have been developed to create the kind of flow that is the key to successful student-led learning. These activities, tools and strategies are suitable for a wide range of subjects and key stages. They are also excellent for pushing students to work at the higher levels of Bloom's Taxonomy.

FOR MORE INFORMATION ...

Stephen Bowkett, *100+ Ideas for Teaching Creativity* (Continuum One Hundred). (London: Continuum, 2007).

Stephen Bowkett, *100+ Ideas for Teaching Thinking Skills* (Continuum One Hundred). (London: Continuum, 2007).

Paul Ginnis, *Teacher's Toolkit: Raise Classroom Achievement with Strategies for Every Learner* (Carmarthen, Wales: Crown House Publishing, 2001).

Geoff Petty, *Teaching Today: A Practical Guide*, 4th edn (Cheltenham: Nelson Thornes, 2009).

For further details of these activities and examples go to:

http://osiriseducational.co.uk/outstandingteaching/resources.

For more Trump Cards activities go to:

http://www.tes.co.uk/article.aspx?storycode=6133685.

Chapter 3

MISS, CAN WE STAY AND FINISH THIS?

WHAT'S IN THIS CHAPTER FOR ME?

■ Would you like to make your teaching easier by not having to constantly coerce students to work?

■ Do you want to be a great motivator of students?

■ Would you like more student engagement and personal responsibility in your classroom?

We sense magic in the air when we walk into the classrooms of teachers who know how to motivate their students. We see their students working hard, enjoying their learning, making progress and above all in flow. To the uninitiated observer it might seem that these teachers have cast some kind of spell over their class, especially when the same students have been observed working with far less enthusiasm and focus in other classes earlier the same day!

Many teachers are unconsciously good at motivating their classes. Ask them how they do it and they won't be able to tell you. The best motivators are often unconsciously competent. The reality is that, consciously or not, they are using a range of techniques which work. In this chapter, we have unpicked the best techniques for you so that you can work this magic on your own classes and consistently raise the engagement levels of all your students.

WHAT'S THE THINKING BEHIND THIS CHAPTER?

Level 1a engagement is typified by highly motivated students. These students are intrinsically motivated and they are finding 'enjoyment of the learning/struggle to learn'. At Level 1b engagement we would expect to see all students 'making significant progress in understanding new ideas/concepts through participation in the classroom activities'. At Levels 1a and 1b engagement students will be leading most of their own learning. This ensures that they are in flow for most of the lesson. The teacher moves from teaching from the front of the classroom for long periods – where students are mainly learning through listening – to becoming an 'activator and challenger' of learners, looking to help students stay on track and to stretch them through questioning and new challenges.

WHAT DO WE MEAN BY MOTIVATION?

To get flow there must be intrinsic motivation. The word motivation comes from the Latin *movere* meaning to move. This is a useful way to think about teaching because teaching is really about moving people. This doesn't mean moving a disruptive student from the back of the class to be closer to your desk (though this might be necessary sometimes), but moving the students you teach towards becoming self-motivated learners who strive to learn and make progress.

The best motivational techniques that teachers use to stimulate their students fall into two specific categories: *extrinsic motivation* and *intrinsic motivation*.

Extrinsic motivation is when motivation comes from the outside. Without that external 'pressure' someone would not undertake the challenge that's been set for them. This form of motivation involves using punishments (sticks) to get less of the behaviour you don't want, or rewards (carrots) to get more of the behaviour you do want. It might also mean deliberately creating disturbance in the students' minds so that they see the benefits of doing things differently.

Intrinsic motivation is when someone does something that they want to do rather than what they are obliged to do. This type of motivation is driven by an interest or enjoyment in the task itself and exists within the individual rather than relying on any external pressure or reward. An example of this is would be when a student does more than the required research because they are so interested in the work.

The bulk of this chapter covers intrinsic motivation, but first let's explore extrinsic motivation.

EXTRINSIC MOTIVATION: 'THE FLYING BOARD RUBBER APPROACH'

In the early 1980s one of us was taught by a particularly strict Music teacher. If he didn't like the way we were behaving he would employ a particularly cheap motivational technique – 'the board rubber'. Off-task behaviour would be punished by the teacher throwing a wooden board rubber at you. Quite a few of us can testify to his accuracy! This teacher got good behaviour from his classes. The flying board rubber was an extreme form of extrinsic motivation.

THE PLACE FOR EXTRINSIC MOTIVATION

All teachers use extrinsic motivation techniques – although the flying board rubber has had its day! Faced with students who exhibit little interest in learning, a teacher may need to use extrinsic motivation strategies, such as establishing rules for working, seating plans, contracts or giving sanctions and rewards. As time goes on the need for these types of techniques should diminish.

A really useful way of thinking about this is the sequence: Contain, Entertain, Enlighten.[1] Teaching others needs to be done in that order because this sequence follows how our brains work. In any new situation we naturally scan for signs of threat. This is a function of the *reptilian* brain, the oldest part of the brain. It is sometimes referred to as the 'fight or flight' response. When students start to feel safe they become more open to being entertained as the *limbic* brain – in particular the hippocampus – is activated. Only after these two stages have been navigated successfully can thinking and reasoning begin to happen. This is a function of the neocortex, the most recently developed part of the brain.

So every September when students arrive in a new classroom with a new teacher, most of them will need to spend some time at the *contain* stage. The length of time they will need to stay there will vary with each class – some will require very little time whilst others might have to remain there for the whole year.

Contain is about establishing positive norms that the teacher wants to see in his or her classroom. These norms – such as working hard, cooperating, reflecting on and improving the quality of one's work – will grow and become embedded over time. One secondary teacher we worked with routinely sets a very complicated homework when he first meets his class. Students who do not give it in on time will get a phone call home to their parents or carers. This sends a tough but very clear message: deadlines are important in my class-

---

1 Ian Gilbert, *Essential Motivation in the Classroom* (Abingdon: Routledge Farmer, 2002), p.155.

room. He won't do this for every homework deadline that is missed, but the students think he will!

In a similar way, enforcing rules such as 'one voice at a time' will help get better quality discussions and more cooperation in the class. With repetition these rules become routine and the teacher has to issue fewer and fewer rule reminders. These norms have to start somewhere. The starting point is the teacher's extrinsic motivation strategies and techniques.

These strategies and techniques do not run counter to the development of intrinsic motivation. On the contrary, when teachers use extrinsic motivation in the right way they create the conditions which *facilitate* intrinsic motivation. These are legitimate forms of extrinsic motivation because they help build learning capacity and establish powerful social norms.

After the contain stage, learners are more open to being entertained. The *entertain* stage involves enjoyment of learning and makes students more receptive to learning. There are hundreds of ideas in this book which have been proven to entertain students and this transforms feelings about learning.

After the entertain stage comes the possibility of enlightenment. This might be thought of as eureka moments where new learning has occurred. The *enlighten* stage is where you will see students making progress and truly in flow.

EXAMPLES OF LEGITIMATE EXTRINSIC MOTIVATION

- Provide clear rules: For participation in class activities we need to be clear about what the rules are. Clarity helps to contain learners and acts as a foundation so that learning can become more entertaining later.

- Set high expectations: Teachers should expect that their class behave and perform at their highest level. When a student falls short of what is expected they will get a punishment ranging from 'the look' to a detention.

  This is the footer that appears on all of Janine Lockhart's worksheets. She consistently gets outstanding judgements about her teaching, great results and is popular with her students. Her expectations are very high and very clear:

I expect 100%, I will accept no excuses. I will not accept sloppy work because I care too much about you. I am willing to discuss any matter with you at 3 o'clock. Work hard! – Mrs Lockhart ☺

- Give rewards: Treats or good work stickers can help a class to get going, but shouldn't become over-relied upon. Some schools have reward systems that students buy into such as points which entitle them to prizes or letters of praise that are sent home.
- Class mantras: Primary teacher Dianne Ryan has trained her class in a number of mantras. When a student is confused in her class this is what you will hear.

Miss Ryan: Are you confused Anna?

Anna: Yes Miss.

Miss Ryan: What do we do when we're confused?

Anna: Work through my confusion, Miss.

All students in this class answer in the same way. Other teachers we have worked with train their students to finish sentences in a similar fashion. Here are some others we've witnessed:

Teacher: Mistakes are what?

Class: Our friends.

Teacher: Because …

The class will give various answers which relate to learning such as 'they help us to learn' or 'the best learning comes after a mistake'. Mantras like these help students to be positive and demonstrate through repetition and good practice how to extend their thinking and become better learners.

In short, some extrinsic motivation is usually necessary. If your class doesn't seem to be highly motivated then you can't simply wait for it to kick in. Teachers need to find ways to make this happen. But the problem with any form of extrinsic motivation is that you, the teacher, have to keep applying it over and over to get your students to *move*. Getting learners into flow requires more than extrinsic forms of motivation. We need to harness the power which is inside all learners – their intrinsic motivation.

INTRINSIC MOTIVATION: 'THE INSIDE OUT APPROACH'

When a student is trying to learn something without being coaxed or coerced by their teacher we can probably assume they are intrinsically motivated. The test would be to say to a class: 'Look, you only have to do this if you want to …' Given this choice, those students who willingly have a go at the activity must feel there's something about it that they'll enjoy or is worth doing. The activity is intrinsically motivating.

Have a look at the following description of a 60-minute Year 8 Science lesson. See if you can spot the *eight* different strategies that the teacher uses to trigger the students' intrinsic motivation.

Lesson objective: Get students to understand the respiration equation and be able to teach others using a variety of media.

Lesson description: Students enter the laboratory and pick up textbooks and exercise books from the front bench. All students are greeted by name. Students copy the learning objective from the board. *(3 minutes)*

Students play a very engaging bingo game which recaps the last homework. Students seem well drilled and they get the answers very quickly. *(5 minutes)*

The teacher moves the whole class to the back of the room where there's a separate whiteboard. Students are each given a written question on a folded piece of paper which has their name on it. They are then put into prearranged groups. The teacher sets each student a mission – to find the answer to their question by the end of the lesson (questions are targeted to stretch each one individually). Each student's target is two-fold: to get a high score in their team challenge *and* to solve their individual challenge during the lesson.

Students are then given instructions about a series of experiments that they will conduct in the lesson. One of these experiments uses cobalt chloride paper. The teacher gets one student to hold it up in the air while another student breathes on it. The paper changes colour. Students see this and are asked to speculate why this is so. *(7 minutes)*

The students then go on to a carousel of experiments to explore challenges such as: Which would you expect to have the higher temperature – air in or air out? Students explore whether they think inhalation or exhalation has more energy. The students carry out further experiments using limewater, thermometers, straws and gas jars, while the teacher's role in the carousel involves her demonstrating an experiment showing how noise differs in air and carbon dioxide. *(25 minutes)*

After the carousel each group of students are allocated some space in the laboratory where their task is to make chalk drawings of the respiratory system on the classroom floor. After 7 minutes each group is asked to present their explanation of the respiratory system to the teacher and other students. The groups are marked for the clarity and accuracy of their diagram and explanation against the success criteria. They are then asked to consider how they had improved on their previous presentation a fortnight earlier using 'two stars and a wish'. This technique invites them to say two ways they have improved and one thing they could do better for their next presentation. *(7–8 minutes)*

In the lesson plenary the students share what they had learnt in the lesson, what questions they still have and what they found the easiest and hardest tasks. Students leave the lesson thanking the teacher and the teacher thanks her students. *(5 minutes)*

Did you manage to detect the eight motivational triggers? This teacher has made the learning *relevant*, *challenging* and *fun*. She finds a way of measuring her students' progress thus building their *competency*. She has also aroused their *curiosity* and *imagination* and offered them some real *choice*. Finally, she has made an effort to build *rapport* with each individual and with the group as a whole.

A breakdown of the lesson illustrating the motivational triggers would go as follows. Students enter the laboratory and are greeted by name *(rapport)*. Students copy the learning objective from the board. Students play the bingo game *(fun* and *challenge)* which recaps the homework *(competency)*. The teacher moves the whole class to the back of the room. Students are given a written question on a folded piece of paper which has their name on it *(rapport)* and then put into prearranged groups. The teacher sets each student a mission and a group challenge *(challenge)*. The teacher demonstrates an experiment with cobalt chloride paper. Students are invited to speculate about the results *(curiosity* and *imagination)*.

Students then carry out a series of further experiments on their own and in their groups *(challenge* and *curiosity)*. Afterwards the groups are asked to demonstrate their findings in creative ways *(imagination* and *choice)*. They then present their explanation of the respiratory system to the teacher and other students *(challenge* and *fun)*. The groups are marked for the clarity and accuracy of their diagram and explanation against the success criteria *(challenge* and *competency)*. Finally, they are asked to consider how they have improved on their previous presentation using 'two stars and a wish' *(competency* and *relevance)*. In the last five minutes of the lesson the students share what they have learnt in the lesson *(competency)*, what questions they still have *(curiosity)* and what they found the easiest and hardest tasks. Students leave the lesson thanking the teacher and she thanks her students *(rapport)*.

This annotation does not fully do the lesson justice. Rapport, challenge and fun were all in evidence throughout the lesson and these triggers were used to get excellent progress (measured against the students target grades for Science).

> In this lesson the teacher used all eight of the motivational triggers. It is not necessary for all the triggers to be used to get high student engagement. However, in our experience of observing hundreds of lessons, we have *never* seen a class of students highly engaged unless the teacher uses a combination of at least *some* of these triggers.

THE EIGHT TRIGGERS

Rapport is about having a connection to or affinity with another person. For many students their level of motivation will be dependent on how much they like their teacher and want to work with them and for them.

Competence can be described as the feeling that students get when they realise that they 'can do'. This feeling raises self-confidence and self-belief, which translates into students being more willing to try new things, learning from making mistakes and stretching themselves.

Curiosity can be aroused in many ways, such as stimulating questions, teases, predictions, wonder and even awe. Writers of soap operas have known for years that if you want viewers to watch the next episode you open up a new storyline, known as a loop or leave the story hanging in the air. The mind likes to close these loops. For many students, stimulating their curiosity significantly increases their engagement.

Imagination is about using creativity, novel ideas or fantasy to transform learning about a topic. When imagination is applied to aspects of learning, such as the context and the resources used, it can lift engagement levels to new heights. As Albert Einstein famously said, 'Imagination is more important than knowledge.'

Relevance is when learning is valuable, worthwhile, useful and useable. It answers the 'What's in this for me?' question which runs through the minds of lots of students. For many of them, seeing real applications of the learning in their lives, whether immediately or in the future, is vital.

Challenge is about overcoming obstacles to achieve desired results. This can appear in many forms. For some it is the burning desire to win (or at least not to lose). It can be a personal challenge such as 'How can I beat my personal best?' Or it could be a challenge to do better than others whether working individually or in a group against other groups. This adds the challenge of working cooperatively as well as competitively, which is also an important life skill. Another form of creative challenge is to invite students to compete against their teacher.

Choice is the cognitive switch from feeling you have to do something (i.e., extrinsic motivation) to wanting to do something (i.e., intrinsic motivation). Rarely can we allow a student to choose to do nothing but giving students a choice of how they do something, where they do it and with what materials can give them a greater sense of control.

Fun is about enjoyment and humour. Most people like humour and some need fun to become engaged with learning something new. According to Edward de Bono, '*Humor* is by far the most significant activity of the human brain.' When some students stop having fun, or don't see the possibility of ever having fun in their learning, they may easily become disengaged.

In the rest of this chapter we want to offer some suggestions about how these motivational triggers can be used. Please note that these triggers are rarely accessed in isolation. We have described them separately in order to give greater clarity.

- Rank the eight motivational triggers from the strongest to the weakest from your own personal point of view.

- Consider that the weakest motivational trigger for you could be the strongest for some of your pupils.

- Start with your weakest trigger and work through the 'how to build' examples of this particular trigger in the following sections.

Set yourself a target to use a personally under-used motivational trigger for a lesson, class or even an individual student that you are working with now.

TRIGGER 1: RAPPORT

Rapport with their teacher is for some students the master key to effective learning. Teachers who are good at establishing rapport get learners on their side quickly. For many students it is their relationships with their teachers that transcends any other factor when it comes to self-motivated learning. The subject matter is always secondary to those relationships.

Establishing rapport with your students does not mean that you necessarily have to like them. Primarily it means opening and holding a channel through which respectful communication and information can flow. During an 'Outstanding Teaching Inset Day' we frequently ask teachers to put up their hands if they ever disliked one of their own teachers so much so that they came to dislike that subject. Over 70% of hands go up. The follow-up question is, 'Who still dislikes that subject today?' Usually around 30% to 40% of hands remain in the air.

This tells us that the personal relationship or feeling you have about your teacher is an important key to unlocking motivation for you and people like you. On the upside, many teachers cite personal inspiration from one of their teachers as a key reason for entering the profession.

The advantages of developing good rapport:

■ Group work is easier because students don't mind who they work with.

■ There are fewer behavioural issues because relationships and respect become established as classroom norms.

■ Attendance and punctuality improve and homework is more likely to be completed on time because students don't want to let you down.

■ Although lack of time is a genuine concern for many teachers, making time to build better rapport with students saves time in the long run. Good rapport between teacher and students is likely to increase learner motivation and engagement. The metaphor changes from battlefield to playing field.

■ Knowing how to work in cooperation with others is a very important ability in most modern working environments.

HOW TO BUILD RAPPORT

RAPPORT-BUILDING IDEA: GETTING TO KNOW YOUR CLASS AS INDIVIDUALS

Teacher Bill Doran holds conversations with his students both formally and informally. These conversations help him gain real insights into their needs. When he became Head of Sixth Form he created a system of reviews which are held once a term. In the reviews, tutors are trained to spend at least some of the time talking to students about their goals, interests and hopes for the future.

Every September without fail, a primary teacher, whose successful lessons we have observed, spends the opening few lessons inducting her class. She uses the Interest Index Card (see below) and closely monitors the responses her students make to the questions. She notes their interests, values and learning styles. As a result she gains valuable insights into what motivates each one. This helps her to personalise examples and generate interest when teaching.

Interest Index Card

What are your favourite hobbies/interests?

What are your favourite television programmes, films, books and songs (three of each please)?

Name three things that you are good at?

Have you got any ideas yet about what career you might like?

What have you learned so far that you find exciting or fascinating?

What are you hoping to learn in this subject?

Note: This is available as a postcard sized template and is downloadable at http://osiriseducational.co.uk/outstandingteaching/resources.

RAPPORT-BUILDING IDEA: COAT OF ARMS

Another way of discovering students' interests is by asking them to design their own coat of arms. This is generally a shield made from canvas, card or paper which depicts six areas, such as favourite hobby, favourite game, favourite place, fantasy song, favourite film and future dream.

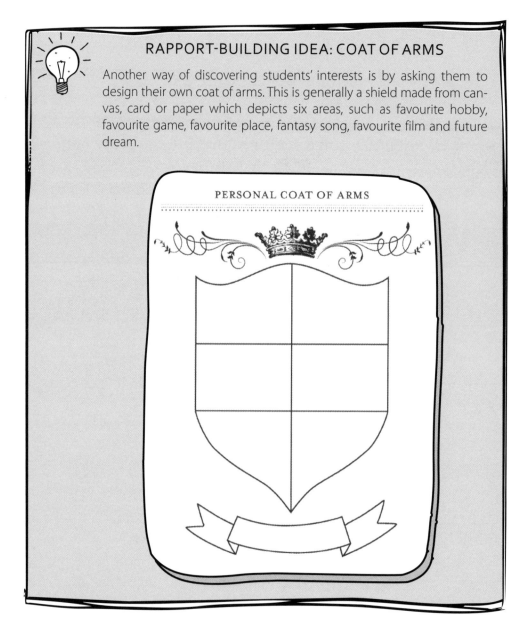

PERSONAL COAT OF ARMS

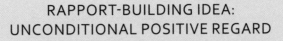

RAPPORT-BUILDING IDEA:
UNCONDITIONAL POSITIVE REGARD

Teacher and motivational expert Paul Kincade believes in taking an unconditional positive regard towards others. He's been using this technique for over 30 years and talks about challenging students as 'rough diamonds'.

Many teachers use this technique without being conscious of it. The term 'unconditional positive regard' was coined by the humanist writer and thinker, Carl Rogers. In his book *On Becoming A Person* (1961) he suggested that it can be most helpful, when working with people you find tricky, to hold them in unconditional positive regard. The fact is, unconditional positive regard is a helpful belief to hold when working with any student, tricky or not.

Thus any teacher who takes a genuine interest in their students, does not hold grudges, regularly uses their names, believes they can do well, works hard to build their confidence and is not afraid to engage in straight talking and honest feedback with them when necessary, is likely to be demonstrating unconditional positive regard.

RAPPORT-BUILDING IDEA:
GO THE EXTRA-CURRICULAR MILE

Why not give some of your time to running a club at lunchtime or after school? This can be anything from a film club to a sports team. Students appreciate this, especially when they don't have these opportunities in their home lives. The other positive side effect is that the students will get to see you in another light. Extra-curricular activities tend to be more of an informal setting and participants choose to be there.

We know a number of teachers who, by adopting the techniques of unconditional positive regard, have transformed their relationships with students. By taking an unconditional positive regard you are adopting an adult stance which helps enormously when dealing with difficult people. Banks, customer service departments and call centres use this technique when training their staff so they can better handle difficult customers. One way to do this in your classroom is to mentally prepare yourself before a lesson. Visualise that 'difficult' student as being brilliant and cooperative today as you walk to the lesson and expect them to be the same for the next lesson because you 100% believe in them.

TRIGGER 2: COMPETENCY

Most student surveys suggest that what they most want from school is confidence. By looking to build a student's competence you will inevitably build their confidence.

The advantages of building competency:

- Letting students know that they are already doing things well and that they are on the journey to their desired destination helps them to remember that they're not starting from scratch. This can frequently motivate them to continue with a challenging task or to reflect on and make improvements to work they thought was completed.

- Students can only really make progress if they know where they are going wrong. Building a 'can do' attitude, sometimes known as a 'growth mindset', can make students more relaxed about owning and sharing their errors and mistakes.

- Getting students to reflect on their achievements helps them to think about what they enjoy most and are best at. This might be an end in itself or, even better, become a career goal.

HOW TO BUILD COMPETENCY

COMPETENCY-BUILDING IDEA: LOYALTY CARDS

Retailers have long known the power of using simple psychology to get consumers to come back to them. For example, the offer of a free coffee once a loyalty card has the sufficient number of stamps is usually preceded by giving customers two stamps on their card to get them started.

At the start of a new topic some teachers make the initial tasks relatively straightforward and achievable so that all students experience the feel-good factor of initial success. This is rather like a sales technique – getting the student 'hooked' by feeling good about the 'product'.

Using similar psychology, RE teacher Rebecca Conn regularly adapts the idea of a coffee loyalty card into a generic activity checklist. Using a grid such as the one below, she lists the tasks that the students have to complete when studying stories and parables from different religions. She makes the early tasks easy so that all students can quickly get a smiley face and the sense that they are on their journey.

Task 1: Design a front cover for your workbook	Task 2: Write an introduction to your work	Task 3: Write a 100-word description of any character	Task 4: Draw and label a character
Task 5: Use a Venn diagram to compare and contrast two characters	Task 6: Compare a character in this parable with another character elsewhere	Task 7: Use five metaphors to describe a character	Task 8: Use five similes to describe five relationships in the story
Task 9: Student choice	Task 10: Student choice	Task 11: Student choice	Task 12: Student choice

Note: This template is downloadable at http://osiriseducational.co.uk/outstandingteaching/resources/.

COMPETENCY-BUILDING IDEA: QUANTITY AND QUALITY OF PRAISE

Very few students complain that their teacher encourages them too much. When Food Technology teacher Sharon Bingham gives work back to her students she only focuses on how they have improved. She uses highlighter pens: green when her students have improved by even 1%; yellow if they have stayed the same. What she also does brilliantly is accentuate these positives with her praise. In giving back a mock exam paper to a student who has gone from 30% to 33% she was so effusive in her praise that this student had a smile from ear to ear.

Use lots of praise and give positive feedback in a variety of ways:

1   Send positive letters or postcards to parents.

2   Give process-oriented praise such as: 'That was a clever way to do that' or 'I like the strategy you are using here'. Try to avoid giving too much person-oriented praise such as: 'You're good at this', 'Good girl' and so on. Behavioural feedback needs to be concrete and give clear guidance for change. It allows every student to earn praise and sells the idea that esteem comes from effort and reflection on what might be the best strategies to improve learning.

3   Use wow! language when you see students doing something that is really helping them to make progress. Words like *fantastic*, *great*, *brilliant* and so on can be applied when you see students working their hardest and making real improvements. However, don't use these words when students are doing the 'basics' (i.e., coming into the room, sitting down, getting a pen out) as at best it lessens the impact of the words and at worst it might come across as sarcasm.

COMPETENCY-BUILDING IDEA: LEARNING LOGS AND PORTFOLIOS

The head teacher of Springfield Special School, John Parkes, is a big fan of using digital portfolios to build competence. The students' portfolios are packed with photographs, exemplar work and in various ways show how over time this student has improved their skills and competencies both as a learner and as a human being.

Portfolios are used in many different professions to showcase skills and achievements. Increasingly, many universities now expect their students to build up a portfolio alongside their studies as it helps them to become more employable and more aware of their achievements.

Students can include anything they wish in their portfolios. It might be as simple as scanning in a piece of writing in September and then doing it again in February to show how it has improved. Or it might involve comparing a video clip of the student's first presentation and then showing a more recent effort of much better quality.

We offer a simple PowerPoint template that students can use to upload achievements. The headings can be decided by the teacher but generally they are along the lines of: What piece of work are you most proud of this year? How have you demonstrated team working? and How have you demonstrated individual initiative? Most students are familiar with PowerPoint. The programme allows pictures and video clips to be uploaded easily and students can use it to support their presentations.

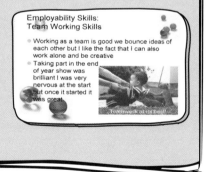

Note: Download different templates and guidance for completing electronic portfolios at http://osiriseducational.co.uk/outstanding-teaching/resources.

TRIGGER 3: CURIOSITY

As human beings we are naturally curious creatures. If we can tap into this innate tendency and capture the interests of our students then we can maximise their interest and engagement.

One Year 5 teacher, Natalie, started a numeracy lesson by informing her class that a chocolate cake had been stolen from the head teacher's office. The students were shocked when they were told that the thief had to be one of the teachers. They were incredibly curious about who it could be. To solve the mystery they had to crack the secret code the thief had left behind.

The teacher commented afterwards that using curiosity had dramatically raised engagement levels.

The advantages of building more curiosity:

- Triggering motivation through curiosity gets students asking questions. Most students ask too few questions. When they do ask questions they instantly become more engaged.

- Curiosity keeps students on their toes. The teacher who uses it is being creative and building the students' creativity too.

- Stimulating curiosity, which may be dormant in a student or teacher, is an essential habit of mind to develop. Students may take their new-found curiosity into other aspects of their lives. As an old Chinese proverb says: 'the quality of your life depends upon the quality of your questions'.

HOW TO BUILD CURIOSITY

CURIOSITY-BUILDING IDEA: USE PROPS

Bringing in interesting objects and resources to the lesson is a great way to arouse curiosity. One teacher we worked with brought in some chicks while she was reading the story of *Chicken Licken* to her pupils. Along with her teaching assistants, she invited pupils into a circle on the carpet and got each child to stroke the chicks and ask questions. The children were already engaged but now they were enraptured!

We often encourage teachers to use props to create more novelty in lessons. Other examples include:

■ *Plasticine movies*: A Science teacher gave her students an interesting challenge on the topic of reproduction. Each group were allocated a window pane, some plasticine and the share of a digital camera. Using resources such as notes and a textbook they had to make a silent movie which showed how a sperm fertilises an egg. Each group presented their movie later in the lesson. Not only that, the class voted for the best movie and the winning group received an Oscar for best film!

■ *The evacuee's suitcase*: Year 4 students walked into the class to see a battered old suitcase in the middle of the floor. First they had to speculate what was in the case and then they got the chance to examine the contents. The suitcase was borrowed from the local museum. To add gravitas to the situation the teacher made the students wear white gloves before they examined the contents which included a gas mask, ration book and so on. The purpose of the lesson was to write a story through the eyes of a wartime evacuee.

■ *Toy cars, chalk and dice*: To explore the topic of probability a Year 5 class was divided into small groups then given 12 toy cars and two dice. After drawing a race track of 10 spaces on the floor, students then numbered each car from 1 through to 12. Students were asked to speculate which cars were most likely to be winners. Students then threw the dice. How many spaces each car moved forward depended on the combined number rolled by the dice. For example, if the dice rolled 2 and 4, adding up to six, car number 6 was moved forward one space. The winner was the first car to reach the tenth space. One would expect car number 7 to win due to the law of probability: seven is the most likely aggregate number to appear when two dice are rolled together. However, not all number 7s won which threw up some interesting questions about the differences between probability and chance.

CURIOSITY-BUILDING IDEA: WHAT HAPPENED NEXT? WHAT HAPPENED BEFORE?

When students are hypothesising and speculating they are working at high levels of thinking. Stopping a story, a video or an experiment to ask students what they think might happen next is another way to get increased curiosity.

A Science teacher used her own personal photos of the Buncefield oil depot explosion in 2005 as seen from her house. She asked students to speculate on what might have caused this plume of smoke. The students then went on to investigate the chemistry behind the explosion.

CURIOSITY-BUILDING IDEA: CREATE A MYSTERY

When a Year 4 class walked into their classroom their teacher, Steve Jones, seemed perturbed. Someone had written graffiti all over the back wall of his classroom! It was a class mystery. Students were used to solving mysteries. They each then went to their drawer and got out their detective badges. It was time for the investigation to begin.

Students devised a plan, interviewed suspects played by other teachers and by a process of elimination worked out who the culprit was. Mr Jones's class clearly love a mystery and have become adept at not just solving them but using them to develop their writing skills. In this case, their task was to write about the case for the local newspaper. For each piece of writing students tried to improve on their previous best work by using better verbs, adjectives, connectives and so on.

TRIGGER 4: IMAGINATION

When a teacher tries something that is novel they encourage an imaginative response. For some learners, being free of the restrictions of traditional thinking awakens their creativity and engagement.

'With your partner, I want at least 20 ideas for how to use this coat hanger – but not to hang clothes. You have two-and-a-half minutes. Off you go!' In this lesson students quickly picked up their mini-whiteboards and were quickly in flow.

The advantages of building imagination:

- Many students love sci-fi scenarios. This can be tapped into by creating problems that need to be investigated and solved on other planets, with aliens and so on.

- Magic has the power to amaze so by applying some of the principles of magic in lessons more engagement will ensue. We're more Tommy Cooper than Harry Potter fans, which reflects our age I guess, but many students love magical stories.

- The future is unknown but by creating future scenarios you can encourage students' agile thinking such as hypothesising and scenario planning.

HOW TO BUILD IMAGINATION

IMAGINATION-BUILDING IDEA: IT'S MAGIC!

One teacher sets her class underway with this instruction: 'You now have in your hand a magic pen but the magic lasts for only 30 seconds. Write down as many ideas about your dream job as you can before the magic runs out. Go!' Any they did – with gusto!

Another teacher has 'magic stones' at hand to help her students. She uses semi-precious stones, the kind that you can get from any visitor centre gift shop, as a way to give her students more imagination. When they are running out of ideas, students ask for one of the magic stones that are carefully locked away in her desk. The 'magic powers' unlock more ideas. This teacher makes a point of giving these stones away when her time with the class has finished. They are sometimes seen in examination halls years later!

IMAGINATION-BUILDING IDEA: SUPER POWERS

In a GCSE Science class, one teacher we observed used superheroes as a way of getting students to understand the relative characteristics and dangers of each of the seven types of electromagnetism. Students were placed in small groups and given information about each of the seven types. Students then had to create a fictional superhero (e.g., X-Ray Man) for one of the types. Each group produced a mask for their superhero which was then modelled by a member of the group. Afterwards these superheroes were hot-seated and questioned by the other groups. The lesson culminated in the class discussing and agreeing the order of the superheroes in terms of their relative power.

> ### IMAGINATION-BUILDING IDEA: SPACE MISSION
>
> An RE teacher created a scenario where students had to select candidates for a mission into space. There were nine candidates initially. Small groups had to whittle the list down to eight, then seven and gradually down to one. After the activity the students had to complete a space mission application form highlighting their own personal qualities.

> ### IMAGINATION-BUILDING IDEA: FOOD IN THE TRENCHES
>
> During an English lesson on First World War poetry, teacher Sayeeda Mahmood had a surprise for her students. A boy came in with a plate of corned beef halfway through the lesson. The corned beef was cut into the exact size of the ration that soldiers were allowed in the trenches. Students who wanted to tried some and then they continued to look at the poetry of Wilfred Owen, Siegfried Sassoon and others.

TRIGGER 5: RELEVANCE

Before some students engage with a piece of learning they like to know that it has relevance to them. When a teacher makes learning relevant it shows a degree of clarity about their subject knowledge but mostly empathy with a learner who is thinking 'Why do I need to know this?'

The advantages of making learning more relevant:

- When students can see the link between the learning and their own lives it encourages them to take more of an interest in the world and be less apathetic.

- Students can see that their teacher is trying to make the learning experience a more compelling one. They will often give their teacher credit for this and will be more engaged.

- When learning is seen as practical and worthwhile it becomes a more personalised experience.

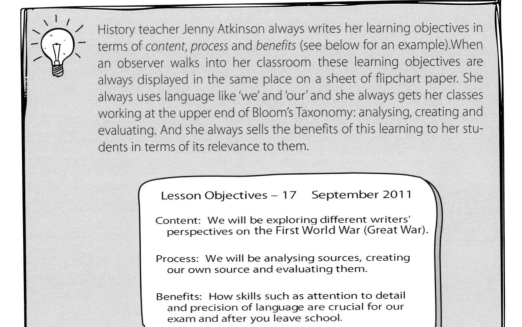

History teacher Jenny Atkinson always writes her learning objectives in terms of *content*, *process* and *benefits* (see below for an example).When an observer walks into her classroom these learning objectives are always displayed in the same place on a sheet of flipchart paper. She always uses language like 'we' and 'our' and she always gets her classes working at the upper end of Bloom's Taxonomy: analysing, creating and evaluating. And she always sells the benefits of this learning to her students in terms of its relevance to them.

Lesson Objectives – 17   September 2011

Content: We will be exploring different writers' perspectives on the First World War (Great War).

Process: We will be analysing sources, creating our own source and evaluating them.

Benefits: How skills such as attention to detail and precision of language are crucial for our exam and after you leave school.

HOW TO BUILD RELEVANCE

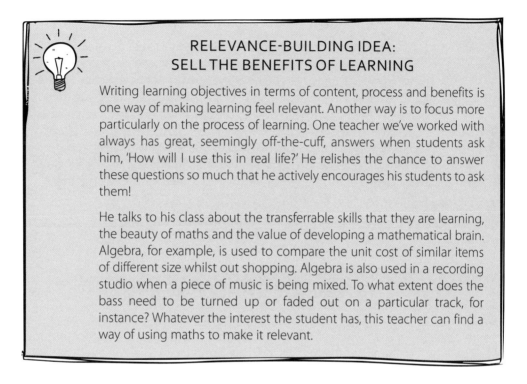

RELEVANCE-BUILDING IDEA:
SELL THE BENEFITS OF LEARNING

Writing learning objectives in terms of content, process and benefits is one way of making learning feel relevant. Another way is to focus more particularly on the process of learning. One teacher we've worked with always has great, seemingly off-the-cuff, answers when students ask him, 'How will I use this in real life?' He relishes the chance to answer these questions so much that he actively encourages his students to ask them!

He talks to his class about the transferrable skills that they are learning, the beauty of maths and the value of developing a mathematical brain. Algebra, for example, is used to compare the unit cost of similar items of different size whilst out shopping. Algebra is also used in a recording studio when a piece of music is being mixed. To what extent does the bass need to be turned up or faded out on a particular track, for instance? Whatever the interest the student has, this teacher can find a way of using maths to make it relevant.

RELEVANCE-BUILDING IDEA:
START FROM EXPERIENCE

Science teacher Jenny Gittins found a clever way of teaching the classification of animal species with a Year 8 class. When students came into the room she asked them to stack their schoolbags into one big pile. She then asked them to 'classify' the bags into five distinct groups.

After a bit of initial confusion the students gradually grouped the bags according to colour, shoulder straps, brands, logos and so on. Afterwards, in small groups, the students were given the challenge of grouping different animals on picture cards into five different categories. There were some tricky challenges, such as the duck-billed platypus and very soon the whole class got into flow.

RELEVANCE-BUILDING IDEA: DESIGN YOUR OWN EXAM QUESTIONS

Teacher Rebecca Graham gets her GCSE students to design exam questions. She gives them a section of a past paper and blanks out some or most of the questions, depending on the group's ability and experience. She then asks them to fill in the blanks. For example, there could be a graph followed by two questions. Students have to predict the aim and wording of the question. The closer they get the more marks they receive. The actual questions and marking scheme are revealed towards the end of the lesson. Students tend to find this strategy hard at first but after they've done a few they get better. Soon they start to feel much more confident about the exam they are going to face.

TRIGGER 6: CHALLENGE

In order to help some students achieve their full potential a degree of challenge is essential. Challenge can be the degree of difficulty. It can also involve competition or the self-discipline of working with others.

In one challenging lesson, we observed students who had to design a quiz which would help the rest of the class revise a topic. In groups of three, students were given some quiz format choices or were invited to create a format of their own. The formats were based around TV quiz shows such as *Who Wants to be a Millionaire?*, *Jeopardy* and *Blockbusters*. Students would challenge at least one other group with their quiz within the lesson.

The advantages of building challenge:

- Some students thrive on competition, either with themselves or others. Other students enjoy the challenge of collaborating in groups in order to create something worthwhile together.

- Challenge can enable you to tie your assessment into whole school systems such as house points. The points systems created for challenging tasks can be linked to Assessment for Learning and can encourage students to make more effort.

■ Challenge that is calibrated to stretch each learner a little bit beyond their current skills level is intrinsically enjoyable, builds their powers of perseverance and fosters flow.

'Okay, everyone settle down. Today is a Challenge Lesson so you know what that means. You will be teaching others today.' This was how one teacher opened her lesson in a Lancashire school where we were working. The teachers have a shared language of 'challenge lessons'. In these lessons, which occur weekly or fortnightly, the students are expected to lead more, create more and teach each other more than in a 'normal lesson'.

HOW TO BUILD CHALLENGE

CHALLENGE-BUILDING IDEA: CHALLENGING LESSON OPENINGS

A thoughtfully prepared challenge at the outset of each lesson gets it off to a prompt and intriguing start. Dingbats, quizzes and lateral thinking puzzles can help students get into the lesson quickly. Competing against others to be the first to solve a problem or beating a previous personal best time to solve these kinds of challenges can be motivating and focusing.

For example: A murderer is condemned to death. He has to choose between three rooms. The first is full of raging fires, the second is full of assassins with loaded guns and the third is full of lions that haven't eaten in three years. Which room is safest for him?

(Answer: The third. Lions that haven't eaten in three years are dead.)

CHALLENGE-BUILDING IDEA:
STUDENTS LEAD PLENARIES

How about getting students into the routine of leading the lesson plenary? In pairs students could be asked to prepare a 3- to 5-minute challenge to check the level of understanding and progress of their peers. Sandringham High School in St Albans uses this strategy during their annual 'Lazy Teacher Week'. They find that it helps students to be more active. After Lazy Teacher Week, where teachers deliberately try to talk less and explain less, the teachers know that they can call on this strategy any time within a lesson because students know different types of plenary activities and have practised delivering them.

CHALLENGE-BUILDING IDEA:
ADD INCREASING COMPLEXITY

Maths teacher Angela Taylor uses mini-whiteboards to great effect in her teaching. In one lesson we observed, her classroom was set up in rows. She asked the students to work out what coordinates they were occupying in the classroom. The girl in the back corner of the room was the origin, 0.0. From that information students worked out their own personal coordinates in terms of where they were sitting.

Later in the lesson, students had to shift their thinking from coordinates and work out the names of students who were sitting on particular lines. For example, who is sitting on the line X=4? She then got the students to stand up to confirm this. She ran these challenges throughout the lesson in between textbook exercises that the students were completing. At the end of the lesson the bell went but was ignored by the class. The students were still trying to work out who was on the line Y=X-4.

CHALLENGE-BUILDING IDEA: TIME PRESSURE

Many students get into flow through being under pressure. Teacher Phil Hayes put his class under pressure in a high-tempo lesson built around a real-life disaster scenario. As students enter the room a video clip of an erupting volcano is playing. Students are quickly allocated into groups of three. Each student is given a sticker to wear and an information sheet to explain their role: information gatherer, team leader, or scribe.

Then a buzzer sounds. The information collector from each group rushes to the class computer where the first newsflash is coming through. Students write it down and return to their group. They then have a decision to make. On their Crisis Management Sheet they have 90 seconds to choose between Choice A, B or C. At the end of the lesson, points are allocated: 10 points for the best choice; 5 for second best; and 0 for the worst choice. The students have 10 decisions to make.

The students loved it. At the end of the activity there was still time for Phil to go through each decision. And he cleverly built in some flexibility over the allocation of points so that if students were able to justify their decision effectively enough they could achieve the full 10 points.

TRIGGER 7: CHOICE

When a teacher offers choice to students it allows them to lead their learning more. Choice is not about opting in or opting out but more about where to start and how you might proceed.

'There are three questions on the board. Start with whichever one you want. Is everybody clear? Yes, then go!'

The advantages of giving more choice:

- Giving choice shows that you are a flexible, trusting teacher. Many students value this quality as it makes for a more relaxed learning environment.

- Some students thrive when you give them choice and a sense of control over what they're doing. Of course they are not in total control, but they have enough to help them feel more engaged.

■ Choice can also give some surprising outcomes. When we invite students to show their learning in a variety of ways, it is not unusual for them to explain concepts more clearly than we did ourselves. The good news here is that we can pinch these ideas for our other classes!

■ Giving students a real sense of choice fosters their awareness of personal responsibility and accountability.

HOW TO BUILD CHOICE

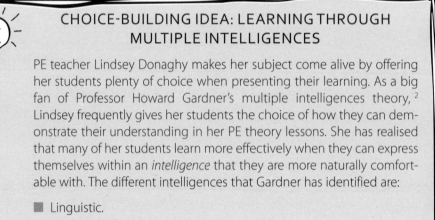

CHOICE-BUILDING IDEA: LEARNING THROUGH MULTIPLE INTELLIGENCES

PE teacher Lindsey Donaghy makes her subject come alive by offering her students plenty of choice when presenting their learning. As a big fan of Professor Howard Gardner's multiple intelligences theory, [2] Lindsey frequently gives her students the choice of how they can demonstrate their understanding in her PE theory lessons. She has realised that many of her students learn more effectively when they can express themselves within an *intelligence* that they are more naturally comfortable with. The different intelligences that Gardner has identified are:

■ Linguistic.

■ Logical/mathematical.

■ Visual/spatial.

■ Musical.

■ Bodily/kinaesthetic.

■ Interpersonal.

■ Intrapersonal.

■ Naturalistic.

Students can choose from among these when demonstrating their learning to each other or their teacher. Below are some examples of activities that stimulate different learning preferences.

2 H. Gardner, *Frames of Mind: The Theory of Multiple Intelligences* (New York: Basic Books, 1983).

Type of intelligence	With this intelligence students like/need to:
Linguistic	Tell or read stories/jokes; play word games; write stories/poems/jokes; debate; hold discussions; write journals; do creative writing; make radio programmes or webinars; take listening roles; do reporting activities; decipher signs and symbols.
Logical/mathematical	Reason; use abstract ideas; play strategy games and logical puzzles; devise experiments to test things out; think in categories and see relationships between ideas; sequence activities; work with numbers to measure, estimate, predict, speculate and hypothesise.
Visual/spatial	Draw, design and build; read maps and diagrams; reproduce images with accuracy; sculpt and model; use visualisation/ imagery activities to stimulate creative writing; play imagination games; use computer graphics; get information from moving or still images; use visual note-taking techniques such as mind maps, concept maps or flow diagrams.
Musical	Use rhythms to produce stories, e.g. through rap music; compose music; recall information using music as an aid; change mood through music; explain through a song/rap.

Type of intelligence	With this intelligence students like/need to:
Bodily/kinaesthetic	Remember through bodily sensations; learn through physical activity, simulation and role play; explore through touch and movement; be involved by moving not just listening; do physical modelling; use body sculpture; do hands-on learning activities; be involved in physical activities such as games/sports/energisers; do Mind Gym exercises.
Interpersonal	Learn by interacting and cooperating with others; lead and organise; pick up on other people's feelings; mediate between people; play social games; listen actively to others; network with others; work with peers; explore emotions through circle time and discussion; play games which develop empathy; be involved in teams; write from another person's perspective.
Intrapersonal	Work alone; motivate oneself; use intuition; develop a sense of independence; set personal goals; be more reflective; become aware of your personal strengths and weaknesses; think deeply about issues; explore personal development issues.

Type of intelligence	With this intelligence students like/need to:
Naturalistic	Make distinctions and notice patterns in the natural world; become more ecologically aware; get involved in farming, pet-keeping, conservation, etc.; become involved in environmental projects; get outside the classroom and into nature; interact with the natural world.

Talk with your class about the concept of multiple intelligences. Ask them to identify their own preferences and share them with you and each other. Invite them to work in groups to explain each type of intelligence and design a lesson around one or more of these. Do the same yourself.

TRIGGER 8: FUN

Most human beings thrive on the pleasure gained from activities which might be described as fun. Teachers should not be afraid to promote fun and allow fun opportunities for learning to take place. Fun can be subjective but most teachers will speak fondly of shared moments of fun with their classes.

The advantages of making learning more fun:

■ A fun environment is normally accompanied by positive classroom relationships.

■ When people are having fun they tend to be less self-conscious. This enables the teacher to experiment with more adventurous forms of learning, such as students writing scripts, producing plays and so on.

■ Plenty of research shows that laughter and fun positively aid learning and memorising.

One teacher uses an inflatable banana called the 'banana of truth'! He throws this around his class and invites the students to catch it. The student is then given a task. For example, answer a question from the teacher or ask another student a question on a nominated topic. This is just one example of how thousands of teachers make their classroom fun places to be. They know intuitively that fun engages their students and makes time pass more quickly for both teacher and students.

HOW TO BUILD FUN

FUN-BUILDING IDEA: SILLY GAMES AND SCENARIOS

One teacher we have worked with has realised that having a few silly games up your sleeve can help you to raise the engagement levels of your class. For lots of ideas on this see the section on 3-Minute Motivators in Chapter 4.

FUN-BUILDING IDEA: GLAD, SAD, MAD

This game is adapted from Rock, Paper, Scissors. Students pair up and then choose three facial expressions to show to their partner: a glad face, a sad face and a mad face. Get students to stand back to back with a partner and give them three attempts to match faces after the count of 1, 2, 3! This is a nice little warm-up game for all ages and can open up a discussion about how the topic makes them feel.

FUN-BUILDING IDEA: KARATE PUNCTUATION

English teacher Conor Rogers uses karate moves to help his students learn different types of punctuation. He stops the class, puts on his bandana (which says 'I love English' in Japanese) and then gets his class to remember different forms of punctuation with appropriate sound effects. For example, a back-to-front 'C'-shaped movement with the arm accompanied by the sound 'swish' represents a comma. This game is also great for getting students to understand mathematical terms such as horizontal X-axis, vertical Y-axis and so on.

FUN-BUILDING IDEA: TEACHER HOT-SEATING

Teacher Rachel Mekonnen likes her students to have fun because she knows that her students will learn better in a relaxed environment. With a next-to-bottom English set she got her teaching assistant to dress up as a witch from *Macbeth*. In role, the 'witch' sat in one corner of the room throughout the lesson where the students asked her questions about the play.

Many teachers we have worked with find value in 'playing the fool' or 'acting the goat'. Whether it's dressing up, doing impressions, working with physical comedy or using facial gestures, these teachers realise that their performance skills help to engage their students and create a learning environment that gets learners easily and often into flow.

FAQS

What is the best form of intrinsic motivation?

There really is no best way to motivate a person. It depends upon the individual. In this chapter we have looked at a number of learning preferences and different personality types and considered various strategies and techniques that will get students more engaged with learning.

How can you work out who is motivated by what?

Barometers such as the one below can easily be used to survey what turns different students on in terms of their motivation. Give these out at the beginning of the lesson and ask students to rate the lesson throughout. Ask students to suggest ways that the learning could have been better for them. Would they have liked more relevance, curiosity, challenge, imagination, competence, choice, rapport or fun?

	5 minutes	15 minutes	25 minutes	35 minutes	45 minutes	55 minutes
Curiosity level						
Comment (optional)						

Note: This barometer template can be downloaded at http://osiriseducational.co.uk/outstandingteaching/resources.

Alternatively, adapt this barometer to a 0 (low) to 10 (high) scale to indicate whether different parts of the lesson are boring or interesting for each student. This can be created as a bookmark and collected in at the end of the lesson.

How will I get time to use all of these motivational triggers?

You don't have to. Start with any of these ideas and run with them for at least a few weeks. Try one of the techniques that you feel will be easier to start with and persevere with it. Check progress with the students and maybe get a colleague to help you 'measure' any improvement in the motivation of the students you are working with.

What's the difference between good extrinsic motivation and bad extrinsic motivation?

It's simply this: if the intention of the teacher is to use extrinsic motivation to help students engage because they feel it would benefit the students then this would show a positive, unselfish intention – that's the good form. If, however, a teacher uses forms of extrinsic motivation that are based on their own personal motives or poor habits, that's where it's bad.

What are the best types of extrinsic motivation?

The best types of extrinsic motivation are usually built around high expectations, clarity and fairness. The best teachers we have observed have very high expectations for behaviour, good manners and above all effort. They express these high expectations in a variety of different ways ranging from sanctions (such as telling-off), punishments (such as detentions) and letters home to parents if the expected standards are not met. They will also model the behaviour that they want to see and set a good example to their students.

Teachers who are clear about what students should be doing and the necessary level they need to be at to do the work competently, are also using extrinsic motivation. They might give written instruction as well as oral instruction as a matter of course or even give a demonstration to students before they begin their work.

Are you saying that you need to be a strict teacher to be recognised as 'outstanding'?

Many students prefer strict teachers, especially when what lies behind this strictness is high expectations and kindness. This is not always the case for strict teachers, but students can soon spot teachers whose strictness comes from more selfish motives. The latter group usually find it hard to get rapport with many of their students.

You don't have to be strict to be outstanding. But we do think that having high expectations for effort and constantly endeavouring to improve the quality of your work are great principles to model to your students. Not pushing our students as hard as we could is a false kindness and helps no one. Most of our students are much more capable than they think they are. And that can also be true for us teachers.

IN A NUTSHELL

Poor student motivation is a real issue for teachers. Extrinsic motivation is often necessary to contain a class and build norms that will help them to become motivated learners. To go beyond the *contain* stage so that learners can become *entertained* and *enlightened*, students need to become intrinsically motivated. Learning which fosters combinations of relevance, fun, curiosity, challenge, rapport, imagination, choice and competence can transform pupil engagement and get them into flow.

FOR MORE INFORMATION ...

Howard Gardner, *Frames of Mind: The Theory of Multiple Intelligences* (New York: Basic Books, 1983).

Ged Lombard, *Motivational Triggers: Motivating the Disaffected* (Trowbridge: Lifetime Careers, 2003).

Carl Rogers, *On Becoming A Person: A Therapist's View of Psychotherapy* (London: Constable and Co., 1961).

Find great resources on motivating the most disengaged students at: www.independent-psychologyservice.co.uk.

We admire the wisdom of Professor Howard Williamson who has led excellent longitudinal studies into the link between social deprivation and motivation. This site also gives information about excellent youth projects around the UK: www.youthstudies.eu.

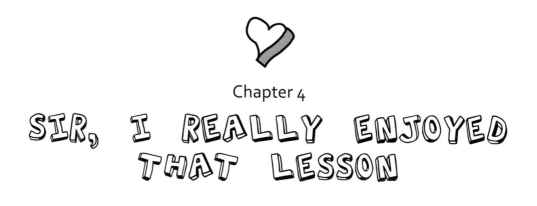

Chapter 4

SIR, I REALLY ENJOYED THAT LESSON

Let's start by asking a simple question: How long would you expect a class of 30 Year 4 pupils, aged between 8 and 9 years old, to maintain concentration? Ten minutes? Fifteen? Try an hour and a half! If we told you that this class seemed to have no real lapses in concentration between registration and morning playtime you might find it hard to believe, but we've got the video to prove it. One primary school teacher on our Outstanding Teaching Programme gets her class into *flow* by exploiting *the power of play*. Her students love her lessons. They also make rapid progress. And this school is in one of the most deprived areas of Liverpool.

WHAT'S IN THIS CHAPTER FOR ME?

- Would you like to create learning environments where your students make exceptional progress, develop great learning skills and exhibit positive attitudes all at the same time?

- Would you like to learn how to transform even the most boring topics into learning opportunities where enjoyment abounds?

- Do you want to become a more playful, less stressed teacher who regularly gets students into flow?

This chapter offers examples of how teachers we've worked with have not only used the power of play to get higher levels of engagement with their students but also more motivation, more involvement, better dispositions to learning and more progress – in other words, Level 1a engagement. It offers a way of teaching that enables us to enjoy our job more and an insight into how being playful can help us to stay healthy and energised.

WHAT'S THE THINKING BEHIND THIS CHAPTER?

During one of our 'Outstanding Teaching Interventions', teachers might find themselves realising that their classes are regularly at a low level of engagement. Assuming that they want to address this situation, we suggest various steps that will help them develop to higher levels. As a reader of *Outstanding Teaching: Engaging Learners*, we hope you will be assessing your level throughout this book and taking and adapting the ideas that will most support you to become more skilful at getting your students highly engaged and more into flow throughout your lessons.

To help you further, let's revisit the highest Outstanding Teaching level for engaging learners, Level 1a. By breaking it down into its different parts, we can then suggest play strategies that will enable you to close the gap between where your class is now and where you would like them to be.

Engaging Learners Level 1a: The students demonstrate that they are *highly motivated and possess excellent learning dispositions*. Students are clearly in flow most/all of the time. The students are highly engaged through their own curiosity and enjoyment of the learning/struggle to learn. The teacher has created a *student-led lesson* (20:80) and acts as activator and challenger. Students are *enjoying opportunities to express themselves creatively in a variety of ways* and are *making rapid progress*.

The sections in italics indicate that at engagement Level 1a enjoyment is high, students have the skills to lead much of their own learning, are working hard and successfully finding different ways to show their understanding. All this is borne out in observations of the class over time that confirm that they are demonstrating all these behaviours regularly and well.

So where does play fit into this? Level 1a engagement describes a class which is cooperative, hard-working, reflective and responsible. Wouldn't it be great if all our students already had these dispositions when we meet them in September? That's not always going to happen. So if you want these dispositions to emerge in your students you will need to do two things: strongly *encourage* these dispositions and *train* your students in them. Both encouragement and training can be delivered by incorporating types of play and playfulness.

Let's remind ourselves of the building blocks for flow. They are that tasks are complex and challenging for each student; that the learning itself is intrinsically motivating; students are clear about what they are required to do and know why they are doing it; they are given the time and space by the teacher to explore the learning; and they get pretty near immediate feedback about how they are doing. Creating a playful classroom can help to strengthen these building blocks, especially those involving motivation, learning dispositions and feedback. Establishing a regularly playful classroom takes practice.

In this chapter we will demonstrate how teachers have used play and playfulness to get their students working at or towards Level 1a.

WHAT DO WE MEAN BY PLAY?

By play we mean a range of active and creative strategies which help students explore and interact with their learning. Play can be planned or unplanned. *Planned play* is when the teacher uses a play strategy in a deliberate way to engage students with what they are learning. The teacher tries to match a play strategy, such as a game, with the learning objectives, seeking a 'best match' to enable the concept to be explored and ultimately understood. *Unplanned play* is more spontaneous; this is where the teacher does things that might be described as 'playful' simply to engage students. An example of this might be using 'misdirection' to challenge students. For example, getting students to copy down a statement and then telling them that it contains three grammatical mistakes. This creates a playful challenge for them to discover what the mistakes are and to correct them. Such games can wake them up and focus them more deeply on their learning. When used effectively methods like these can deliver hard and fast results. In short, play is a serious business!

HOW DO I BUILD PLAY INTO MY CLASSES?

Even the most intransigent teenager was once a baby who explored their world through play. All students and teachers for that matter, know what play is; it's just that some of them have forgotten how to do it. Playful students need to be comfortable:

- Working cooperatively.
- Practising different ways of expressing their learning.
- Being open to sharing learning, including their mistakes.
- Reflecting on their own learning.

The higher you can build these skills with your students, the more they will be able to lead their own learning.

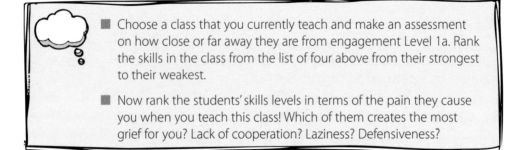

- Choose a class that you currently teach and make an assessment on how close or far away they are from engagement Level 1a. Rank the skills in the class from the list of four above from their strongest to their weakest.

- Now rank the students' skills levels in terms of the pain they cause you when you teach this class! Which of them creates the most grief for you? Lack of cooperation? Laziness? Defensiveness?

Creating a cooperative class environment underpins high engagement. Your students will want to help each other and they'll feel more relaxed, safer and be willing to work harder because they don't want to let down their classmates. Cooperation develops when there has been a build-up of sufficient trust between the students and their teacher and between the students themselves.

Three great playful techniques to help build cooperation are:

- Clear rules and expectations.

- Warming students up to play.

- Playful ways to get attention and allocate tasks.

CLEAR RULES AND EXPECTATIONS

Students value clarity and fairness. When playing a game, for instance, don't expect your class to be mind-readers! Be explicit with the rules. Without clear rules, that you enforce fairly, some of the stronger personalities in your class will try to dominate activities at the expense of other students. Some games can get very lively as points start to rack up and competitiveness sets in. Be careful that your rules mean that everyone gets a fair go.

'Work Hard, Be Nice' is the slogan of the KIPP (Knowledge Is Power Program) schools network in the United States. We like the simplicity and clarity of this. You don't have to use these rules but whatever rules you do use, make them short and clear. 'Working hard' and 'being nice' means different things to different people. De-mystify this by having discussions and then getting consensus with your students about what this means. 'Effort levels', such as those discussed in Chapter 5, are a great way of doing this, as is the following exercise.

> Ask a student to go the side of the room and invite them to see how far he or she can reach up the wall. Tell them to 'do your best'. Wait until they have just returned to their seat and then ask the same student to return to the wall and 'Now *really* do your best'. Just before the student gets back to his or her seat call them out again. This time get the class to chant the student's name as they jump up the wall to reach a higher point. You will then have three marks on the wall, each higher than the last. The message is clear: if you push yourself and if we push each other, we can go to higher levels.

WARMING STUDENTS UP TO PLAY

To work together at high levels students often need brief warm-up games which require cooperation. For example, when English teacher Anne Riley wants her class to learn through role play she uses some warm-up games first to build cooperation. Anne realises the importance of games such as the ones below:

■ *People to People* – ask students to find a partner and get them to stand 'back to back'. Once in this position give them instructions to follow as quickly as possible, such as 'hand to hand', 'hands to shoulders', 'elbows to elbows', 'hands to elbows' and so on. When you say 'people to people' students have to find a new partner. This game can be made even more fun by highlighting the poor listeners and even booing them back to their seats. Only do the latter, of course, after you've established trust in the classroom and the good-natured context of the game. The tone needs to be right.

■ *As One* – give students instructions that require them to stand up one at a time but in no prearranged order. Sounds easy, except as they stand they must shout the next number in the sequence. So the first person says 'one' as she stands up, the next 'two' and so on. However, if more than one student stands up and shouts the next number at the same time the class have failed to work 'as one' and have to start all over again. This game teaches students that when there is clear communication it's a lot easier to succeed.

■ *Team Circle* – get students to form a tight circle (or series of tight circles), with each person facing the back of the next person's head. Then ask them to simultaneously sit on the person's lap who is behind them. This will not work unless the class cooperates and communicates with one another.

Anne Riley knows that when she wants her GCSE English students to act out a scene from *Romeo and Juliet* she has to warm them up first. She gets students to simply walk past each other. Then she asks them to walk past each other and make eye contact. And then she asks students to walk past each other with a swagger. She gradually builds engagement before any dialogue from the script is spoken.

PLAYFUL WAYS TO GET ATTENTION AND ALLOCATE TASKS

You can often tell an excellent teacher by the absence of wasted time in lessons. We offer you some ideas for getting tasks underway quickly and allocating roles efficiently. Many teachers who start to use these techniques immediately see the benefits. More time is found for students leading their learning, more time for reflection and a few laughs along the way.

One teacher we worked with in a London primary school has a very playful way of getting attention. She has realised that there are more and less effective ways of getting attention when she wants to give out instructions for a task. So rather than raising her voice and commanding her students to 'Listen', she gives them something playful to do instead. This has the advantage of waking them up without any resentment towards her. One way she does this is by using an auditory cue. She gets her students rhythmically clapping their hands to a quick catchy tune. This signals that it's time to look at the teacher and pay attention.

Other good-humoured ways of getting attention include using auditory cues such as a small bell or even simple things such as: 'OK, everyone put your index finger in the air. Everyone, point at the window, point at the ceiling, point at something which is blue, now point at me. Drop your fingers but keep your eyes on me. Now what I want you to do is …'

10-second games are games that take 10 seconds or less to decide winners and losers. The power of these games is that they are fast, quirky and subtle. They wake up your class and get them down to work quickly. Their apparent randomness helps prevent resistance and gets students quickly involved. Many teachers have found these simple techniques to be great ways to get activities underway quickly, find group leaders, re-group students seamlessly and get more energy into their classroom. Very few resources, if any, are needed for these games.

Some examples of 10-second games:

- Roll a dice – 'Person with lowest score goes first'.

- Place your palm on your partner's palm – 'Whoever has the biggest fingers goes first'.

- Rock, Paper, Scissors – 'Winner chooses to go first or second'.

- All the group stare at each other and don't blink – 'First one to blink is your group leader who will feed back your group's ideas'.

- Compare house numbers – 'Highest goes first'.

- Think of a favourite animal – 'Person with fiercest/cutest/biggest animal goes to join another group'.

- Pick up a playing card – 'Highest card is group leader'.

- Spin a pen – 'Whoever has the nib of the pen pointing at them is team scribe'.

When this random way of allocating roles is embedded in your class there will be less resistance and visibly more cooperation.

HOW TO USE PLAY TO GET YOUR STUDENTS TO REFLECT ON THEIR LEARNING

Reflection is vital for learning. Not all students are naturally reflective so finding ways to build this habit will help more of your students remember their learning and realise what gaps exist in their understanding.

Three great playful techniques to help build reflection are:

- 3-Minute Motivators.

- Playful questioning.

- Memory games.

3-MINUTE MOTIVATORS

The phrase '3-Minute Motivators' was first used by Kathy Paterson in her book of the same name.[1] These games are used to great effect by teachers who notice that the class needs a short but positive break from the current routine in order to refocus and get remotivated. They are also an excellent technique to help students review their learning. This could be as simple as using a game like 'verbal tennis' for three minutes before bringing students back to the topic. In verbal tennis, students sit facing each other and try to score points by coming up with words within an agreed topic such as film titles or colours. As soon as hesitation or repetition occurs the opponent wins the points. This can be easily adapted to any topic to help students review learning, even from several months earlier.

3-minute motivators have a number of advantages: they show pupils that the teacher is good at noticing when students are not engaged; they help create a playful classroom atmosphere; and they offer positive 'carrots' to students for persisting with something that they find difficult. 3-minute motivators tend to be memorable. They act as anchors that can help participants recall what was learned and they can help energise or refocus individuals in the group. The structure of introducing 3-minute motivators to students has been adapted from Kathy Paterson's book:

Step 1: Cue to gain attention. The best way of doing this is some sort of agreed auditory signal such as clapping hands or ringing a little bell or gong. Whatever your chosen cue, the students must give you their full attention within a few seconds.

Step 2: Explain why the motivator is being used. 'Thank you class. Now, you seem a bit sleepy/distracted today so let's use a 3-minute motivator to get you more focused.'

Step 3: Explain the 3-minute motivator. 'I want you to find a partner and stand up facing them.' Wait until all students have a partner and allow a three if necessary. 'Now let's play Questions Only. You get a point if your partner hesitates, repeats an answer or answers a question. First to get three points wins. Go!' Model this if you need to.

Step 4: Stop or change the 3-minute motivator. Always use a cue to do this. For example, you might decide that you want to use a 3-minute motivator to recap previous learning. In the example of Questions Only you might say, 'OK, new game. Keep going with the questions using the same rules for scoring points as before, but now you must only ask questions to do with this topic. First to three points wins. Go!' You might want to get the students to change partners as you switch the activity.

---

1 K. Paterson, *3-Minute Motivators: More Than 100 Simple Ways to Reach, Teach and Achieve More Than You Ever Imagined* (Markham, ON: Pembroke Publishers, 2007).

Step 5: Conclude and refocus by summarising what was done and why. 'Great. We just played Questions Only. You seem a bit more focused now. Let's get back to our learning.'

Here are some examples of 3-minute motivators:

THE UNINVITED GUEST

Science teacher Jill Ealey likes to give her students the challenge of demonstrating a concept through play acting. For instance, a student might be asked to step outside the classroom. As the student goes out, the teacher gives them a secret task on a folded piece of paper. For example, 'You are magnetic!' The student returns and behaves as if they are attracted to any metal objects in the room. The rest of the class have to guess what they are trying to demonstrate. She then makes this tougher and tougher by getting students to pretend to be elements or compounds.

PICTIONARY

Pictionary is a game where people take it in turns to draw a picture and the other players try to guess what it is. Normally they have only a minute to do this. A Year 4 teacher we worked with provides cards with key learning ideas for each topic. Students come up and try to draw what's on the card. If the drawer doesn't understand what's on the card the teacher can whisper some suggestions. The student who guesses the correct answer from the drawing goes and gets the next Pictionary challenge from their teacher. This game can be adapted all the way up to degree level for nearly any topic.

GUESS WHO (OR WHAT)?

A Year 1 teacher we worked with used sticky labels to get students to deepen their understanding. A note containing words or shapes is stuck on a student's forehead or back and the student has to guess who or what they are by asking questions of the rest of the class. The only answers that are allowed are 'yes' and 'no'. This game benefits both the guesser and describer. For example, when trying to guess shapes students might ask 'Do I have four sides?', 'Do I have more than one symmetrical line?' and so on.

5, 4, 3, 2, 1 ARTICULATE

Science teacher Anna Russell uses the game Articulate as a way of getting her students to review their learning. First she writes a list of key terms and concepts on the board. Students then form pairs and are given a topic. Each partner now takes turns to talk about the topic for 60 seconds whilst the other has their back to the board. Then they swap seats. Each time they mention one of the key terms listed they score a point. For a competitive edge, the class can be divided into two teams and friends may give advice if the student in the hot-seat is struggling.

SNOWBALLS

Primary school teacher Joanne Stewart introduced her Year 5 class to the game of Snowballs to get more of them asking questions. She brought in a big box wrapped up as a present and gave each student a piece of paper on which they had to write their name. On the same piece of paper she then asked the students to write some questions in silence about what they thought might be in the box. After 30 seconds the students were asked to screw their piece of paper into a 'snowball' and throw it in the air. Each student then had to find another snowball, unwrap it and add to the questions. They did this a number of times before each paper was returned to its 'owner'. During a game of Snowballs each student receives back a piece of paper with a lot more questions than they started with. After such a fun, physical way of generating questions, students find that they are more open to analysing their original questions and then encouraged to share the questions on their sheet verbally with the teacher and/or their classmates.

PLAYFUL QUESTIONING

Questioning does not need to be predictable and boring. How about trying some of these ideas?

THE QUESTIONING SCARF

After watching himself teach on video, Sherlon Atkins realised that he needed to do something different to get all his students to engage in questioning. He decided to get them involved by having them catch a scarf that he had tied into a ball. The 'questioning scarf', as it became known, was soon a regular feature in his classroom and it significantly helped Sherlon's students to listen better and participate more.

ROLLERBALL

In a Year 3 class, one teacher created a novel way of getting students to answer questions. She uses a panelled football which the class call 'Rollerball'. On each panel she has written a different question which get students to reflect on their learning. When the Rollerball emerges from under the teacher's desk the children call out 'Rollerball, Rollerball, roll, roll'. If the ball lands at a student's feet they are given plenty of time to think of an answer or make a contribution. If they still cannot answer they roll the ball on to another student.

SPEED DATING

A Year 6 teacher used Speed Dating to gauge what the students had learned from the topic. Students sat facing their partner in two concentric circles. They each then had a minute to say what they knew about the topic or to raise any questions. After one minute the teacher rang a bell and each player in the outer circle moved one chair to their left to face a new partner. The pair work was repeated three more times before the students went back to their normal seats. During the activity the teacher had written down on one side of her whiteboard 'what we know' and on the other side 'what we're not sure of'. She then filled in the columns with the help of the class. This game provides a safe environment for students to share their questions and any gaps in their knowledge. Finally, the teacher asks what other questions they have from their conversations with their classmates. Getting this information helped her to skilfully restructure the remaining part of her lesson.

MAGPIE CARDS

Primary school teacher Mark Radforth makes questioning very playful in his classroom. Amongst his many techniques to get questions and answers from his pupils are Magpie Cards. When students are working on a group activity they will have a laminated picture of a magpie in their pack. When Mark shouts 'Magpies!', selected students have a few minutes to visit other groups and 'steal' ideas. This works well when the group activity is something visual such as posters, graphs and so on. The students who have used the Magpie Card return to their groups and share the stolen ideas/facts with their team.

META-COGNITION DICE

To improve her students' reflection skills, languages teacher Siobhan Doris uses meta-cognition dice. She makes large, blank, foam dice or dice from paper or card, that don't make a sound, and writes questions like these on them:

- How could you have learned this faster?

- How will you remember this for your exam?

- What skills have you been using as part of this learning?

- What part of the assessment criteria are you covering?

- How could you use this learning outside of this subject?

- How confident are you at explaining your learning?

Teachers can also use their own meta-cognitive questions. Used regularly they tend to build the habit of getting students to reflect not just on *what* they are learning but *how* they are learning and *how well* they are learning.

MEMORY GAMES

Pairs is a card game in which all of the cards are laid face down on a surface and two cards are flipped face up at each turn. The object of the game is to turn over pairs of matching cards. The winner is the person who can match the most cards. This game can be easily adapted for matching a word and its definition, a fraction with its equivalent decimal, a character with a quote, a year with an event and so on. This game is best played in a group of three allowing one of the students to play the role of referee who, with a sheet of answers, can confirm or deny whether the other students have matched the right cards. Students can also be asked to use the structure of Pairs to create their own game to test others in their class.

Map from Memory is an activity where learners recreate a map of information using their short-term memory. This works as an excellent activity to recap prior learning either to start a topic or as a revision task. It is a great way to promote talking and listening amongst learners as they try to plug the gaps in their own map. The way it is structured prevents excessive teacher talk because their role is simply to introduce the activity and then act as timekeeper for each round. Students are put into groups of three. Each one is given a number: one, two or three. The teacher calls up all the number ones. These learners have got up to 30 seconds to study a diagram or map. They have to memorise as much as they can before they return to their group where they verbally explain what they can remember to the other two. Another member of the group then starts to create a picture from the description that the first person has given them on the team's large piece of paper. The process is then repeated with the number twos going up, having a 30-second viewing time before returning to their group and so on. The aim is to recreate as accurately as possible the map or diagram. Just about any diagram, such as a mind map or a flow chart, would be suitable for this activity.

Mnemonics are devices to help us to remember. They can be found in different subjects where using a rhyme such as 'I before E except after C' can help us to remember an important spelling rule. There are also spelling acronyms, such as Not Every Cat Eats Sardines (Some Are Really Yummy) for the word necessary. List order acronyms help us to remember, for example, the order of sharps in music (the 'circle of fifths' – F, C, G, D, A, E, B) as Father Charles Goes Down And Ends Battle. And in reverse, for flat keys, the mnemonic can be neatly reversed: Battle Ends And Down Goes Charles's Father.

Rhymes, spelling acronyms and lists can be taught to students to help them remember. Getting students to create their own is an even better idea as students might suggest acronyms that become even more memorable for the whole class.

- Are all your students reflective? How good are your students at reviewing their learning outside of lessons?

- What more playful methods of teaching could build the habit of reflection in your classroom?

- In what topics could you use 3-Minute Motivators, playful questioning or memory games to encourage your students to review their learning?

Try a few playful questioning techniques such as 3-Minute Motivators or memory games to explore whether they really do help your students review and remember their learning more effectively and in a more engaging way.

HOW TO USE PLAY TO GET YOUR STUDENTS TO EXPRESS THEIR LEARNING

Albert Einstein once said: 'If you can't explain it simply, you don't know it well enough.' Understanding is different from just knowing. It involves being able to move beyond repeating knowledge 'parrot fashion' and going to a deeper level of engagement with the subject matter. A good test is if you can take new learning and teach it or explain it to someone else. The phrase 'understanding performances' was coined by Professor David Perkins to describe a set of activities which force students to explain their learning through a variety of different expressions.[2]

Three great playful techniques that help express learning are:

- Quirky 'understanding performances'.

- Classic games.

- TV show formats.

---

2 David Perkins 'Teaching for Understanding' in *American Educator: The Professional Journal of the American Federation of Teachers*; v17 n3, pp. 8, 28–35, Fall 1993.

QUIRKY 'UNDERSTANDING PERFORMANCES'

Creating situations where students have to explain learning in quirky, often humorous ways, develops their skills of analysis, evaluation and creativity as well as providing memorable learning.

RAPPING

This challenges students to distil and refine their knowledge into a new form and pushes them to move to a deeper level of understanding. One Science teacher we saw needed his AS Chemistry class to more deeply understand a particular topic so he set them the challenge of creating a rap to explain different aspects to fellow classmates. Before they attempted theirs, he played a short video of himself doing a rap on the topic! Students had 12 minutes to prepare their rap. Rappers were then questioned by fellow students and the teacher to ensure that they really did understand what they were explaining. The teacher then set his students some past examination questions on the topic.

TWITTER

The online social networking site Twitter gave Law teacher Sarah Sakalas a great idea for a Twitter-style 'understanding performance'. Twitter users send and receive text-based posts up to a maximum of 140 characters; but in this case it was on mini-whiteboards rather than online. Halfway through her lesson on sentencing policies, she asked her students to tweet a summary of their learning so far. This enabled her to see very quickly which students were not yet certain about the distinctions between the different types of sentencing. The quirkiness of this activity got all students highly engaged and helped them to learn from each other's interpretations of the topic.

REWRITE A SONG/CREATE SONG LYRICS

Rewriting a song allows students to 'play' with vocabulary by substituting their own words in songs. Either provide a choice of song titles or get students to choose their own. One teacher we know regularly challenges his students to use music from iconic TV shows such as *EastEnders*, *Coronation Street* and *Match of the Day* to get his students to apply and perform different topics within the framework of a well-known tune.

PHYSICAL JERKS

One Science teacher we've worked with got her students to demonstrate their learning about the behaviour of atoms with movement. They had to physically demonstrate how atoms behave in a solid state: static and vibrating; in a liquid state: attached and moving between each other; and in a gaseous state: running around all over the place. Noticing just how much her students enjoyed learning this way and how well it stayed in their memory, she now regularly asks her classes to demonstrate understanding in a physical way. For example, demonstrating the flow of electricity around a circuit or how cancerous cells attack healthy cells. In every case, her students express themselves physically then explain their performance in the spoken or written word or both.

FOOTBALL COMMENTARY

Ask students to summarise their learning in the form of a football commentary.

ANGRY LETTER OR ARGUMENT BETWEEN TWO PEOPLE

Ask students to summarise their learning either as a letter of complaint or as an argument between two people. After this written exercise, they then present it to the class – with anger!

COMIC STRIP

Ask students to summarise their learning in the form of a comic strip. Get students to display and then explain how their comic strip develops. Try http://comiclife.com/.

For all of these 'understanding performances' students will need time to prepare. It's also a good idea, when introducing these ideas for the first time, to model the kind of 'understanding performance' you're looking for or give a few examples. After they've presented, invite students to assess whether the performance has been informative as well as entertaining. It's great to see a student getting up and performing, but sometimes fellow students can be so busy laughing that they miss the learning opportunity. So make sure this is covered in the lesson debrief. Other useful ideas for the debrief are to challenge the performers to explain why they chose the particular words they used and to ask the watching students to rate the usefulness of each performance in terms of it helping their understanding of the topic or as a revision aide.

CLASSIC GAMES

We define a classic game as one which has stood the test of time and whose rules are easily understood and employed. Below are some examples of games that we are confident will still be around albeit in other formats for many years to come.

CONNECT FOUR

This is a well-known game which involves players taking it in turns to place different coloured counters into a frame. The goal is for two players, taking turns, to connect four discs of their colour in a row (vertical, diagonal or horizontal). Below is an example of how a Maths teacher has adapted this game to help students to practise rounding numbers (decimal places and significant figures). In this version the students play in groups of three – two play against each other and the other is the referee and timekeeper. In a set amount of time, such as 20 seconds, each student has to complete a sum. If it's judged as correct it can be highlighted with the colour they have been given. If they don't get it right the square is left as it is. The other player can now attempt this square or another one. If they get their answer right they can then highlight it with their colour and so on until one player gets four in a row.

Connect Four

345 to 1sf	0.079 to 2sf	3.999 to 2 dp	0.07049 to 3sf	451 to nearest hundred	300.28 to 1 dp
302 to nearest hundred	699 to 1 sf	994 to 2 sf	76.045 to 3 sf	20785 to 3 sf	0.40404 to 4 sf
0.00790 to 3 sf	2.596736 to 2 dp	0.00060 to 2 dp	1299 to the nearest thousand	0.00060 to 2 sf	78.065 to 3 sf
65.4 to 1 sf	799.09 to 4 sf	4882 to 2 sf	586.50 to 3 sf	73.009 to 3 sf	1459 to the nearest thousand
23408 to 2 sf	68574 to 2 sf	0.5004 to 2 sf	456.348 to 2 dp	48593 to 3 sf	2001 to 2 sf
0.000015 to 1 sf	76.5030 to 4 sf	4509 to the nearest thousand	2.3436 to 3 dp	76.059 to 2 dp	675.468 to 2 dp

SNAKES AND LADDERS

This is another classic game that encourages students to learn through play. Snakes and Ladders is a board game where players roll dice to try to get from the start to the end of the board. Along the way they will face both snakes and ladders. The former will entail sliding down to a lower square whilst landing on a ladder elevates you up the board.

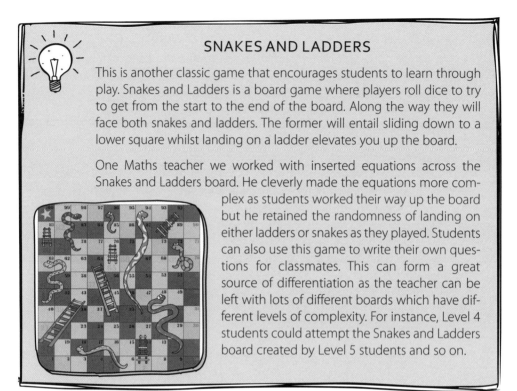

One Maths teacher we worked with inserted equations across the Snakes and Ladders board. He cleverly made the equations more complex as students worked their way up the board but he retained the randomness of landing on either ladders or snakes as they played. Students can also use this game to write their own questions for classmates. This can form a great source of differentiation as the teacher can be left with lots of different boards which have different levels of complexity. For instance, Level 4 students could attempt the Snakes and Ladders board created by Level 5 students and so on.

With a little imagination both *Connect Four* and *Snakes and Ladders* can be adapted for many purposes, not just Maths. Students can create their own questions to embed in the games and challenge their classmates. The skill of creating a game requires the application of their learning and they will likely ask tougher questions than their teachers will! An important rule if you do this: students must know the answers to the questions they set.

TV SHOW FORMATS

Popular TV shows can also form a great structure for students to play with. One teacher we worked with told her students that they were going to be pitching their ideas as if to the Dragons on *Dragons Den*. Being familiar with the game the students fell into the roles very quickly and used language and phrases from the show such as, 'I will offer you the full £100,000 for that idea …'

In fact any TV show that students enjoy can be reproduced in the classroom. The most usable types of programme include reality shows, quiz shows and chat shows. Chat shows with celebrity guests have been popularised by Oprah Winfrey, Graham Norton and others in recent times. History teacher Cassie Evans uses this format to re-enact historical events. For example, the host calls on his first guest: it's Henry VIII. After a short interview, the host then introduces Anne Boleyn. The students who role play these characters have to carefully consider how these two would interact with each other, what their body language would be like at certain stages in their relationship and so on. Another teacher we have worked with uses the pre- and post-match TV interview that so many students, especially boys, are familiar with. Assisted by a toy microphone the teacher interviews historical characters such as King Harold before he goes into battle with William of Normandy. Of course it will only be William who has a post-battle interview!

The more popular the format with the students, the more likely they are to buy into the game.

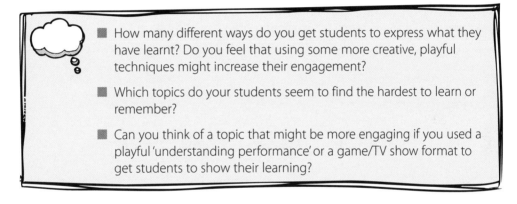

- How many different ways do you get students to express what they have learnt? Do you feel that using some more creative, playful techniques might increase their engagement?

- Which topics do your students seem to find the hardest to learn or remember?

- Can you think of a topic that might be more engaging if you used a playful 'understanding performance' or a game/TV show format to get students to show their learning?

Try a more quirky, playful 'understanding performance' and get feedback from the students in terms of their enjoyment and increased level of understanding. Be inventive with these formats.

HOW TO USE PLAY TO GET YOUR STUDENTS TO BE OPEN TO SHARING THEIR LEARNING AND THEIR MISTAKES

Misteaks are crucial to learning! When a student realises they have made a mistake it can enable new learning to take place. However, many students try to hide their mistakes thus preventing progress. These students regard making errors as a sign of failure. Others are so serious about doing well that they tense up and become defensive about sharing their mistakes and misconceptions. When teachers successfully turn these attitudes around, getting their students to own their mistakes and current limitations, their students can make much quicker progress.

Three great playful techniques to build your students' openness are:

■ Rewarding mistakes and errors.

■ Modelling playfulness.

■ Using humour.

REWARDING MISTAKES AND ERRORS

It is essential that students feel their classroom is a safe place. Not just a place where they can learn, but crucially where they can make mistakes without fear of ridicule. After all, learning can be a messy business. We rarely move directly from not knowing to knowing. We have to go through the process of meta-learning: the messy stages in between what we can do now and what we'd like to be able to do in the future. For this reason, discomfort and disturbance are necessary aspects of new learning. They indicate firstly that the student is engaged in the process of change (learning is a change process) and secondly that the teacher is doing her job by challenging the students to move out of their comfort zones.

Students are much more likely to take the kinds of risk that enable accelerated learning when they feel secure. It makes them much more open to speculating, hypothesising, creating and being open to sharing and expressing their learning. For this reason many outstanding teachers find that playful ways to reward and incentivise students to take risks can be really helpful.

Maths teacher Alison Ashton takes her students through a popular ritual when they realise they have made a mistake. She literally asks individuals to get up from their seat, take a penny from a pile that she keeps in the top drawer of her desk and then drop the penny into a piggy bank that she keeps on top of a filing cabinet. She uses the pennies to buy sweets for the whole class at the end of each term. This ritual shows that Alison values her students sharing their errors and the whole class gets rewarded for spotting them and helping each other to find and learn from these mistakes.

MODELLING PLAYFULNESS

Another way of creating learning environments where students are open to sharing their mistakes can be fostered through the playful demeanour of the teacher. These are teachers who take a relaxed approach, who join in with play, who use their voice to build suspense, who show enthusiasm by being childlike and who look for opportunities for having fun. Playfulness can include being silly if you teach younger children or, with older students, perhaps pretending you have lost your voice so that they are required to teach the lesson for you!

THE ART OF DECEPTION

You don't have to be an illusionist like Derren Brown to influence another person's thinking. Using the amusing and engaging strategy of deliberate deception can really help a class to develop deeper understanding and take greater responsibility for their own learning and thinking. Using body language cues, such as nodding your head while explaining a deliberate falsehood, can be one way of achieving this.

Languages teacher Claire Malone regularly uses the art of deception in her teaching by setting Class versus Teacher challenges. When the class win a challenge they get a point; if she wins the challenge the teacher gets the point. For example, Claire might point to a series of pictures on a screen and then ask the class to repeat after her. If she points to a chair and says 'chaise' and then the class chant 'chaise', the class gain a point. If she points to a window and says 'fromage' and the class stay silent, the class again get a point. However, if just one student says 'fromage' out loud the teacher gains the point. Unless, of course, there actually is a piece of cheese stuck on the window. The first to five wins.

Getting students to deliberately create wrong answers and play against other teams in the style of *Would I Lie to You?* or *Call my Bluff* can also deepen understanding.

USING HUMOUR

Many teachers use humour to encourage their students to feel relaxed and to build class identity. They also use comedy to let their students know that they don't take themselves too seriously. As G. K. Chesterton once wrote, 'Angels can fly because they take themselves lightly; devils fall because of their gravity.' So when equipment fails to work and things go wrong, the teacher who maintains their sense of humour tends to get better rapport with students. The main forms of humour used by teachers tend to fall into three categories: *figural*, *verbal* and *physical*.

Figural humour usually includes cartoons and comic strips. Giving students a comic strip to start a lesson and asking them to create new captions (or the other way round) can be an effective way of getting students to create a fun and engaging start to the lesson. The whole class can judge the funniest ones at the midpoint or end of the lesson.

Verbal humour is about wordplay and can stimulate students to better comprehend language-based incongruities. There are various forms of verbal humour including jokes, parody and funny stories. Verbal humour is a big part of British culture particularly in the forms of stand-up comedy and television sit-coms. Those teachers who use verbal humour well can foster a lot of energy in their classrooms.

Physical humour is highly visual. It includes behaviour which might be described as clown-like such as slapstick, mime, facial gestures, body language and comical movements.

- How do your students feel about making mistakes and sharing their mistakes?

- How do you or can you, use play to get your class more relaxed about sharing errors and misconceptions?

- What can you do to improve your own personal playfulness?

> How can you find more ways to use humour in your classroom by looking for more opportunities to find it in your daily life? The development of a sense of humour is more than just the ability to tell a joke. Choose the type of humour that you are comfortable with, but remember that humour is a social phenomenon. It is for sharing with others, so don't be afraid to consider new experiences that might broaden your humour horizons.

In addition to the play strategies that we've suggested above for developing more effective learning habits, also consider some of the following strategies:

Let your students know that you value play

Make sure your students know that you value play and find ways to convince them, if they need convincing, that play can help them to learn. Use the language of 'play' (which usually has positive connotations) instead of 'work' (which can have negative connotations). Use phrases like: 'Play around with those ideas for a few minutes …' or 'Let's play this strategy game and see what we discover …' The metaphors we use can have a big impact on the atmosphere we create in our immediate environment.

Find out how your students like to play

Talk with students about play in their lives, for example, computer games, board games, outdoor games, card games, sports, dance and music. Find out their likes and dislikes to get an insight into their play habits and preferences.

Cooperation and competition

The games and activities in this chapter are mainly cooperative in nature. If they do have a competitive element it is in the spirit of challenge rather than there being any sense of 'losing'. Competitive games with points systems can be used and have their place in motivating students. However, if games are used to eliminate people – 'you're out' type games – they can create barriers between classmates and losers may feel disappointed, angry and devalued.

Be clear to students why you are asking them to play

It is important to plan well the games you intend to play in class and be up-front with your students about your reasons for using them. The role of the teacher is to ensure that educational play has a purpose and structure. The purpose being to engage students to make progress with their learning. It is not just there to fill time.

Ignore these ideas at your peril. Play tends to be the most natural and most memorable of all learning methods. Closing your mind to play also closes off the possibility of your students getting into flow. A playful classroom may not necessarily be rated as 'outstanding' all the time, but it can form the foundation for students enjoying the challenge of trying to achieve the very best progress that they are capable of. For us that's what being outstanding is all about.

FAQS

Won't more play compromise my exam results?

Most teachers have a packed syllabus and pressure to get their students through all of it. Yet a playful classroom can still be a place where students make exceptional progress. In fact we think that play might even enhance exam results! When playing a game, students can be presenting, explaining, debating, judging or even hypothesising. When play stimulates such skills these students will not only be in the upper part of Bloom's Taxonomy, they'll be breaking through it! Remember A and A* grades at GCSE and high grades at KS5 can only be attained when students demonstrate skills like synthesis, analysis and evaluation.

Won't more play give students more opportunities to misbehave?

Some teachers worry about introducing elements of play into lessons because they fear that it will create classroom chaos. In Chapter 3 on motivation we talked about the sequence of contain, entertain and enlighten that enables learners and teachers to move towards outstanding teaching and learning. A playful classroom can enable each of these three stages to develop. When we've spoken to teachers about their fear of using more play and playfulness, the typical response is anxiety about the class becoming 'out of control'. But when we look closer, it's not the whole class that is the problem, but more usually the behaviour of two or three difficult students. By deciding not to be in any way playful with your class, this means that those difficult students effectively win. They are setting the classroom norm which becomes 'we don't play here'.

Establishing the right boundaries and rules for students to work and play within massively reduces opportunities for misbehaviour.

So start by establishing clear rules and then use the tried and trusted techniques of:

- Class contracts – get a written agreement about rules that all students agree to. These can be the school rules or your own version which complement these.

■ Proximity – stand closest to your 'usual suspects' or those who have a propensity for being silly, uncooperative and so on.

■ Refocus – for example: Karl is talking to another student and isn't participating. Teacher notices and says, 'Karl, what should you be doing?' Wait for Karl to reply with, 'Helping to prepare the presentation.' To this you reply, 'Come along then Karl, thank you.'

■ Opt out – in some cases it is appropriate to allow students to opt out of the activity. They need to be given alternative work to do which requires them to sit at a desk and not interrupt others.

Some of my students can't play or won't play – what should I do?

Dealing with reluctant players is often at the forefront of teachers' minds. We have some great examples of how teachers can successfully get these students more involved. It's strange that those students who don't seem to want to play in class will often spend a lot of their leisure time playing! In fact, many students will get into flow in their lives outside school through various forms of play. We just need to break down whatever their barriers are.

Some students will openly say that they don't feel like playing a game, so be patient. Getting a class to achieve beyond its expectation is a long-term endeavour, but always leave the door open for them to play. We're not fans of having deep conversations with students about why they are resistant to playing. Just give them the option of joining in when they wish or give them something else to do which keeps them involved with learning.

One useful strategy for getting the resistant-to-play students on board is to ask others in the class what games those students do enjoy. Then see if you can find ways of adapting those games to your teaching. Or just offer your students a no-brainer frame: 'Which would you prefer, a bit of learning with a few games or straight exercises from the textbook?'

According to Brian Sutton-Smith, 'the opposite of play isn't work. It's depression.'[1] When a student doesn't play at all you should speak to someone in the pastoral team of your school as they may need to be referred to a counsellor or mental health professional.

We believe that play can be great therapy for the unmotivated student and we have offered many ways to get students playing in this chapter.

I'm not a very playful person so how can I encourage my students to be playful?

We believe that everyone likes to play, albeit in different ways. It could well be that you hold a belief that play and playfulness is about having a whacky sense of humour and

---

1 H. E. Marano, 'The Power of Play' in *Psychology Today*, July–Aug 1999, pp. 36–42.

being clown-like. Although play does sometimes take this form, we realise that our suggestions in building play must fit into your style of teaching so that you can maintain your personal authenticity. We've packed this chapter with ideas that will suit different personalities, different topics and different ways of learning.

What would an Ofsted inspector say if they saw me using lots of play when they came into my lesson?

The days of the showcase lesson are over. It's best not to think in terms of an occasional lesson observation but more about the sort of positive norms that you want to create in your classroom to help students learn. Any person coming into a playful classroom will see high amounts of engagement, challenge, cooperation, feedback and, above all, progress.

IN A NUTSHELL

Play is a serious business. Encouraging play and playfulness will help students not only get more enjoyment from their learning but also more progress. Using playful methods in our teaching can get students to be more alert, more interested, more engaged and into more flow. Play can also become a desirable habit for both teachers and students, enabling them to value playful ways of exploring learning and living.

FOR MORE INFORMATION ...

Guy Claxton, *Hare Brain, Tortoise Mind: Why Intelligence Increases When You Think Less* (London: Fourth Estate, 1997).

Robert Fisher, *Games for Thinking* (Buckingham: Nash Pollock Publishing, 1997).

Malcolm Gladwell, *Tipping Point: How Little Things Can Make a Big Difference* (London: Abacus, 2000).

Daniel Goleman, *Emotional Intelligence: Why it Can Matter More Than IQ* (London: Bloomsbury, 1996).

Keith Johnstone, *Impro: Improvisation and the Theatre* (London: Faber and Faber, 1979).

Pat Kane, *The Play Ethic: A Manifesto for a Different Way of Living* (London: Macmillan, 2004).

Kath Paterson, *3-Minute Motivators: More Than 100 Simple Ways to Reach, Teach and Achieve More Than You Ever Imagined* (Markham, ON: Pembroke Publishers, 2007).

Brian Sutton-Smith, *The Ambiguity of Play* (Cambridge, MA: Harvard University Press, 1997).

Link to more than 300 ways to turn learning into 'understanding performances':

http://legwork.pbworks.com/w/page/16185298/Ideas%20for%20the%20As%20Pot%20%20200%20ways%20to%20show%20what%20you%20know/.

The Pre-School Learning Alliance, an organisation which encourages the growth of play in schools:

www.pre-school.org.uk/.

Montessori schools are play-centred learning environments. Find out more about them at: www.montessori.org/.

Robert Fisher's website with great resources and ideas:

www.teachingthinking.net/.

Dr Stuart Brown's talk linking play and flow:

http://www.ted.com/talks/stuart_brown_says_play_is_more_than_fun_it_s_vital.html.

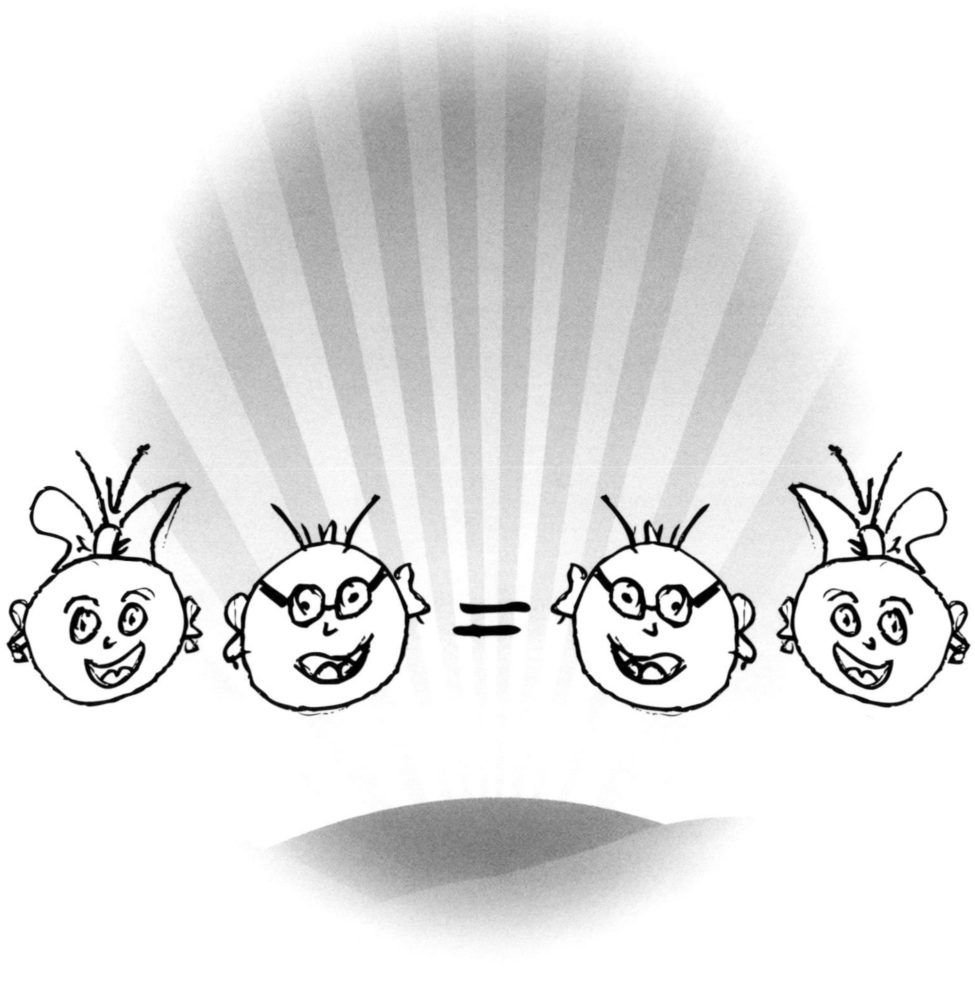

Chapter 5

IS THIS THE SAME CLASS AS LAST TERM?

Teacher: Why aren't you completing the work?

Student: CBA.

It's very sad when a student is so unmotivated he can't even be bothered to say that he 'can't be arsed'! It seems to us that there's an epidemic of unmotivated young people in our society. As trained secondary school teachers, we used to think this was a problem limited to children of 11 years and over. But our recent work in primary schools suggests that this is a false premise; even here there are pupils who've developed the habit of not trying. Depending on the way they exhibit their poor motivation, these students can make our jobs even harder. For many teachers, poorly motivated students are their number one problem.

There's also the problem of poor learning skills. Even the best teachers will struggle to get an 'outstanding' judgement if their students lack the necessary skills to make progress. We know that having a child in your class who is unmotivated and/or has weak learning skills can be an exhausting experience.

WHAT'S IN THIS CHAPTER FOR ME?

■ Do you want to understand the common reasons why some students don't engage with their learning?

- Are you curious about what your classes might look like if your students were trained to become more engaged in their learning?

- Would you like to be a teacher who is known for transforming students' knowledge, attitudes, skills and habits?

If you're interested in finding ways to change the mindset of your students then this chapter shows you how to do it. We know it's hard enough to change your own thoughts and behaviours, even when you want to, but trying to change the thoughts and behaviours of students who apparently 'can't be arsed' can be a massive challenge. However, we can help by giving you the tools you need to address many of the poor habits that your students have developed.

WHAT'S THE THINKING BEHIND THIS CHAPTER?

It is often said that we are living in the Information Age. As Ian Gilbert explores in his book *Why Do I Need a Teacher When I've Got Google?* (2010), the teacher's role as the font of all knowledge is an old-fashioned view of teaching. Students need more than just being able to get knowledge from their teachers. What they need is a teacher who can develop in them the skills, attitudes and habits that can support them to thrive in the modern world.

Many of the suggested techniques in this chapter require the teacher to also take on the role of 'trainer', motivating their students to develop more effective practices, behaviours and thought processes. Only by accepting this as an indispensable part of their teaching brief will teachers be able to tackle the low motivation that exists in so many classrooms. It's essential that teachers support their students to work smarter and more cooperatively and to take more responsibility for their own learning if outstanding teaching and learning is to take place.

KEY REASONS FOR LOW ENGAGEMENT

In our experience the main reasons for students' lack of engagement fall into the four areas of Knowledge, Attitudes, Skills and Habits (KASH).

Students lack the 'right' knowledge

In order to make progress, students need to know their current level of performance. They therefore require accurate knowledge of their level of performance. Highly engaged students also know where they want to go with their learning – they know why they need to persist, to take advice, to work hard. This is because they are working towards a personal goal. We find it interesting that of the thousands of students we have taught it is not necessarily those with the most problematic lives that are the most disengaged. It's true that some students have had traumatic experiences in their young lives, but this doesn't have a direct causal link to the student's ability to become highly engaged. Actually it's the knowledge of how to put those issues behind them and stay in the moment that determines their ability to focus.

▨ Students lack the 'right' attitudes

Some students can't or won't come on a learning journey with their teacher. We do not mean specific learning difficulties or even physiological factors (e.g., poor sleep patterns or a poor diet). What we're talking about is learned behaviour in relation to their beliefs about themselves and their attitude to the way, in their view, the world works. One such attitude that can develop is *learned helplessness*. Learned helplessness is a term first coined by psychologist Martin Seligman and it refers to a set of pessimistic thoughts that the person holds to be true.[1] These thoughts often harden into limiting beliefs, especially in relation to 'trying'. Students with learned helplessness believe that they will fail and so see no merit in persisting or taking chances. This is where the 'What's the point?' attitude can develop.

▨ Students lack the 'right' skills

For a class to be regularly working at Level 1a/1b, it's essential they have the right skills. They require individual skills, such as expressing themselves clearly, listening actively, reflecting on their learning and understanding what they have to do to improve. They also require the skills of working with others as learning takes place within a social context.

▨ Students lack the 'right' habits

A habit is best explained as having the ability to do a task without any conscious thought; it becomes routine or as we call it a 'norm'. We know that if we reflect on ourselves for a few moments we have a mix of both good and bad habits. When it comes to how our students behave in our classrooms we can also appreciate this mix of good and bad learning habits.

We say at various times throughout this book that it is crucial to 'start with the end in mind'. We have taken this directly from Stephen Covey's influential book *The 7 Habits of Highly Effective People* (1989). It seems to us that teachers who regularly get judged as 'outstanding' have got into the habit of starting with the end in mind. Because they are clear about

---

1 Martin Seligman, *Learned Optimism: How to Change Your Mind and Your Life* (New York: Simon & Schuster, 1991).

what norms they are looking for they spend time training their students in the underpinning knowledge, attitudes and skills required for them, if necessary, to change their habits.

Let's contrast the KASH of students who have been judged to be at engagement Level 3 compared to Level 1a.

Level 1a	Level 3
Knowledge Students are clear about what is expected from them (the product of their learning) and they are clear why they are learning this knowledge (the goal of their learning). They can see 'the big picture'.	**Knowledge** Students are on task but are unclear about what is expected from them (the product of their learning) beyond the actual task that they are doing. They are unclear why they are learning this knowledge (the goal of their learning) – they lack the 'big picture'.
Attitude Students embrace a variety of active learning challenges and 'understanding performances'. They have a 'can do' attitude.	**Attitude** Some students resist attempts by the teacher to get them more actively engaged in their learning; others are trying to learn or being compliant.
Skills Students are almost completely independent of the teacher. The class are an effective group. They work well as a unit and individuals thrive.	**Skills** Students are dependent on the teacher. The class do not work well with their teacher or each other.
Habits Students persist when tackling a complex task. They have developed the habit of leading large parts of their own learning.	**Habits** Students give up easily when tackling a complex task. They have not yet developed the habit of leading large parts of their own learning.

■ Who in your class gives up too easily?

■ Who resists trying new ways of expressing their learning?

The following exercise illustrates a profound point about how attitudes are formed and changed:

Step 1: Picture a student who has low motivation. Get that student's face fixed in your mind before you move on.

Step 2: Look at this picture of a baby.

Now consider that the student you're picturing was once a cute little baby just like this one. They'll have explored the world with a similar curiosity and sense of adventure, taking countless risks in the pursuit of knowledge and understanding. And, even if only to lay hands on the rusk on the table across the room, they'll have set off, fallen down a few times and struggled to reach it. But they'd never have given up. No baby gets halfway across the room and stops to think, 'I can't be arsed to get that.'

Step 3: Next time a student 'presents' with signs of being unmotivated remember that this is learned behaviour. And anything that is learned can be unlearned.

Step 4: Consider this: you have only two choices with these students; there is no third way. You can either do nothing or you can take action. Waiting for these students to transform by themselves is not a viable option. In the vast majority of cases it simply won't happen.

THE JOURNEY FROM LEVEL 3 TO LEVEL 1

If you want to help your students become more motivated, rather than just accepting them as they are, you might be curious to read how a teacher can move his or her class from a low to a high level of engagement in just a few short weeks.

In the rest of this chapter you'll find proven strategies to build the attitudes, skills and habits of your learners. All these strategies require that you *train* your students to develop the skills and attitudes that will help them thrive at engagement Level 1a – a high level of challenge and independence, where problem-solving and persistence are essential characteristics of getting into flow. In particular, we need to explore strategies that support your students to:

- Cope with being stuck.

- Do their best.

- Work as part of a group.

TRAINING YOUR STUDENTS TO COPE WITH BEING STUCK

One area where teachers have really developed their students' motivational strengths is training them to welcome and work through 'being stuck'. If students are to make progress and achieve their learning goals it's essential that they build capacity to overcome the hurdles in their way. Being stuck can feel like a disaster or a sign of failure on their part. In extreme cases some students will throw down their pen and simply withdraw from the challenge.

The fact is that being stuck is a necessary and normal part of most learning experiences. We just have to work through it. Challenge and stuckness are essential elements for getting into flow. It's therefore important for students to have a toolkit to get themselves unstuck. Here are a range of techniques that outstanding teachers frequently use to help their students deal with being stuck or confused.

STUCK BOARDS

Primary teacher Clare Gore has become a big fan of using stuck boards in her classroom. These are laminated cards printed with statements like these:

We're great learners

When we're stuck we keep trying and we:

Try breaking the question down into smaller parts.

Try another question and come back to the question we're stuck on later.

Try having a go on a whiteboard first.

Highlight the bits we find difficult or the key words.

Look at our working walls and displays.

Clare and other teachers like her train their students to use their stuck boards to develop new routines when they get stuck. The boards challenge them to use a range of strategies before asking for help and encourage the learners not to give up. The statement at the top of the board is important too. 'We're great learners' is both an affirmation for the students and shows that their teacher believes in them.

WONDERWALL

Humanities teacher John Brown has created a great routine for getting his students to share questions. He's created a space in his classroom  which he calls the Wonderwall. Here students can place questions on sticky notes throughout the lesson. He trains his students to share these questions without any fuss. When students are tackling their work John can look at the Wonderwall and then speak to individuals or groups to help them with their question.

HELP DESK

A help desk or help station is easy to set up in any classroom. It has helped Textiles teacher Karen Dobie to transform her lessons. A help desk can be as basic as allocating a desk in a corner of the room where extra resources – such as books or a computer connected to the inter-net – provide students with additional support throughout the lesson. Teachers like Karen encourage their class to use this area as a matter of routine. It's really impressive when you see students accessing the help area without needing to ask their teacher for permission. These students have developed the habit of trying to solve problems for themselves without recourse to their teacher.

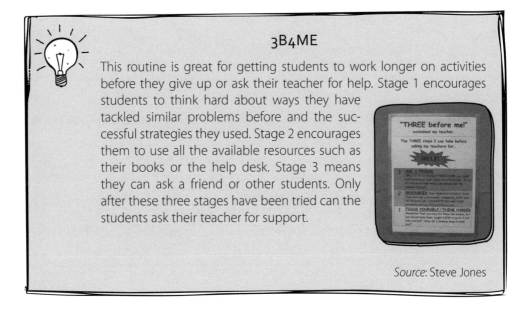

3B4ME

This routine is great for getting students to work longer on activities before they give up or ask their teacher for help. Stage 1 encourages students to think hard about ways they have tackled similar problems before and the successful strategies they used. Stage 2 encourages them to use all the available resources such as their books or the help desk. Stage 3 means they can ask a friend or other students. Only after these three stages have been tried can the students ask their teacher for support.

Source: Steve Jones

TEACHING STUDENTS UNIVERSAL TRUTHS ABOUT THINKING

A universal truth is something that is always true, everywhere. These truths cross time, borders, genders and cultures. Some people say that there are no universal or absolute truths. A good question to ask those who believe this is: 'Are you absolutely sure of that?'

Before we get too deep, see if you agree or disagree with these 'universal truths':

■ Square sandwiches never taste as good as triangular ones.

■ People who don't drive slam car doors too hard.

■ The first person who tried to steal your nose was your uncle.

■ Occam's razor is fine but not as good as a Gillette.

■ Nothing sounds more fun than the sound of a primary school at breaktime.[2]

---

2 These 'truths' were all sourced from www.boreme.com.

We're not sure if these statements are universally true. They certainly can't be proven. However, the next set, about how our minds work, may be (scientifically) provable. Do you agree or disagree with the following statements?

1   Even in the most extreme circumstances a human being can still choose his or her actions.

2   The mind can have a powerful liberating influence on our potential but also a powerful limiting influence too.

3   Each person creates their own thoughts and they can change the way they think.

EVEN IN THE MOST EXTREME CIRCUMSTANCES A HUMAN BEING CAN STILL CHOOSE HIS OR HER ACTIONS

We who lived in the concentration camps can remember the men who walked through the huts comforting others, giving away their last piece of bread. They may have been few in number, but they offer sufficient proof that everything can be taken from a man but one thing. The last of his freedoms – to choose one's attitude in any given set of circumstances, to choose one's own way.

Viktor Frankl, *Man's Search for Meaning*[3]

We cannot control events but we can control our responses to them. Explore different scenarios with students and let them discover that there is never just one way to respond to events. In teaching this principle to students we like the equation $E + R = O$ (Event + Response = Outcome). The Event is always constant because we have no control over it but our Response can change. Let's look at this in another way. If a student insults you or your family this is an Event and there are a range of responses available, not just one or two. Exploring these through discussion or even role play encourages students to become option thinkers.

---

3 V. Frankl, *Man's Search for Meaning: The Classic Tribute To Hope from the Holocaust* (London: Random House, 1959; first published in German in 1946 under the title *Ein Psycholog erlebt das Konzentrationslager*), p. 86.

THE MIND CAN HAVE A POWERFUL LIBERATING INFLUENCE ON OUR POTENTIAL BUT ALSO A POWERFUL LIMITING INFLUENCE TOO

What is true, definite or certain to one person can be the complete opposite to someone else. 'Maths is easy', for example. Students come to us with different beliefs. Some of those beliefs, such as 'I can learn anything if I put my mind to it', are helpful for learning and developing relationships. Other beliefs, such as 'I'm not clever enough to do this', are limiting and create obstacles to learning and relationship-building. Explore students' beliefs with them. This is best done in one-to-one interviews or through a survey. Encourage them to choose helpful and empowering beliefs. This can be best achieved with a whole class who come to an agreement such as: 'We work with our teacher and each other to do our best'.

EACH PERSON CREATES THEIR OWN THOUGHTS AND THEY CAN CHANGE THE WAY THEY THINK

Thoughts grow with attention! They can exaggerate situations. While an actual event, such as an argument with a friend, can last a minute or two, your mind can recreate that event, magnify it and make it last three hours – or an entire lifetime. If you identify a student who tends to think very negatively then here are some strategies you could helpfully teach them:

▓ Become aware of your negative thinking habits

One way to break an old habit of negative thinking is to replace it with a new habit of letting go of negative thinking. This may involve asking a friend to monitor your thinking by keeping a log of your negative comments for at least two days. Keep a piece of card with you with the words 'What am I thinking right now?' written on it. Look at this card regularly and talk to your friend who is helping you to observe your thinking to realise the extent of your negativity. If you or the person monitoring your thinking decides that you are being too negative then you can go to the next step.

▓ Learn to ignore your negative thoughts

Once you realise that you do a lot of negative thinking, what can you think instead? The answer is that it doesn't matter. As you catch yourself thinking negatively just let that thought go and you will find that your mind will be much clearer and freer than it ever has been before. Other thoughts will naturally fill the space. When a negative thought does come into your mind, let it pass by. Don't give it the time of day. Remain uninterested in the negativity.

> For students to make progress they have to go beyond their current knowledge, skills or mindset. Do you provide sufficient strategies for your students to stick with complex problems?
>
> Negative mindsets are a serious block to effortless learning. Think about ways to challenge your students to frame their thinking in more positive ways. Help your students understand that we all generate our own thoughts and we can choose to hold on to them or let them go.

> Try one of 3B4ME, stuck boards, help desk, wonderwall or teach your students some universal truths. Give it at least four weeks and see how the *norms* for independence in your class have changed.

TRAINING YOUR STUDENTS TO DO THEIR BEST

In your teaching do you value effort as well as achievement? Many teachers say they do, but when they properly analyse their teaching they realise that they could do much more to get their students to try harder. Not everyone can get top marks for a writing assignment, so creating an environment that also rewards those who try the hardest means that encouragement, progress and improvement are at the very heart of your teaching.

DESCRIPTIVE PRAISE

Descriptive praise is one of the most powerful tools to encourage your students to make more effort. Every time you notice students doing something well, give them descriptive praise. This simply requires you to describe accurately back what you saw him or her do and then explain clearly how they will benefit from the action they took. It sounds straightforward but it's notoriously hard to do. We've all heard the advice that we should offer four times as much praise as criticism, but few teachers can maintain that level of positivity. Nevertheless, when we do it, it can transform students' engagement.

To praise descriptively, find a positive action an individual or a group has taken. Describe back to them what they did. This could be how they behaved, how they studied or how they interacted. Don't eulogise or judge in any way. Merely describe as accurately, simply and succinctly as you can exactly what they did.

Now add one further sentence describing the benefits of this action for themselves and others, for example:

- ▪ I noticed the way that you listened to other people's views before giving your own. That makes them more willing to listen to your views and improves the quality of conversations.

- ▪ You sat still for that entire activity. That made it much easier for the other students to include you.

- ▪ I saw that you didn't give in during that entire problem. That kind of persistence encourages the rest of the group to get to the answer.

> There are many things you can choose to praise: student behaviour, mastery of a skill, a positive attitude or a good learning disposition. It will depend on what is currently important and appropriate for you and your students.

>
> Descriptive praise takes time to master but the benefits are enormous. Try it with one class for four weeks. Give no criticism, lots of positive encouragement and smiles and let rip with lots of descriptive praise!

EFFORT LEVELS

Another way of getting your students to make more effort is to be clear about the differences between trying a little bit and trying a lot. Why not experiment with 'effort levels'? These can help students realise that they alone are responsible for the effort that they put in.

The beauty of effort levels is that they remove any delusions that students might have about whether or not they really are trying hard. When you ask students to try their best it will mean different things to each one. Effort levels allow us have classroom conversations such as:

Teacher: What level of effort are you working at Alison?

Alison (after a pause to read levels): Probably level 4 Miss.

Teacher: What can you do to get to level 2?

Effort levels and descriptors can usefully be accompanied with imagery and metaphors to make it more fun and engaging. For example, level 7 effort could equate to a white belt in karate, whereas level 1 would compare to a black belt. No doubt you can find many other metaphors that would be appropriate to the interests of your students. Effort levels put responsibility for personal effort onto the student themselves. When students get to co-create and agree on these levels and their accompanying metaphors, they can be even more powerful.

Effort level	Effort descriptor
Level 1 (Excellent)	I am working as hard as I possibly can. I am working as hard as I do when I am doing my most enjoyable pastime.
Level 2 (Very good)	I am trying very hard and pushing myself to be better. It's not quite my very best effort but not far off it.
Level 3 (Good)	I am trying pretty hard when working but not as hard as I do in other subjects. I am taking a degree of pride in my work.
Level 4 (Satisfactory)	I generally participate in learning activities and I do what I am expected to do by my teacher. I do not go beyond anything that I am asked to do either in class or for homework. I use the minimum amount of effort to get by.
Level 5 (Mediocre)	I make some effort some of the time but only when I have to. I am punctual most of the time but I need frequent reminders from my teacher to stay on task.

Effort level	Effort descriptor
Level 6 (Poor)	I rarely make any effort. I regularly turn up late to the lesson and rarely have equipment (e.g., a pen) that I need with me.
Level 7 (Very poor)	I make no effort at all in lessons. I never arrive on time or have equipment (e.g., a pen) with me.

Note: You can download effort level descriptors to use in your classroom at http://osiriseducational.co.uk/outstandingteaching/resources.

■ Do all your students understand the same thing when they are asked to 'do their best'?

■ Can you think of a metaphor that your class might buy into which links in with the effort level descriptors?

Experiment with effort levels for one of your classes. Give some time to linking the levels to a metaphor and talk through it with your class. Try it for as few weeks and see if your students start to work harder.

TRAINING YOUR STUDENTS TO WORK AS PART OF A GROUP

Engagement Levels 1a and 1b describe the characteristics of excellent learners as:

■ Students accept one another and are comfortable to express themselves, take risks and ask questions.

■ Students take responsibility for their own learning and behaviour.

■ Students cooperate with their teacher and with each other so that everyone supports each other to make the best progress they can.

■ Students confront problems and challenges with a resilient attitude.

Groups like this don't just happen – they have to evolve. Like children maturing step by step into adulthood, groups also have to be carefully nurtured towards maturity. At each stage of their journey, a person or a group has to learn to cope with new problems and develop new skills and attitudes in order to overcome obstacles and challenges. It is this process that helps the individual or the group to reach a more mature stage of development. In the case of a group we want them to become a productive working unit which takes learning challenges in its stride.

The following section shows you how to get your students working at these higher levels of engagement in the shortest time possible.

ALWAYS START WITH THE END IN MIND

Taking your class through a formal and rigorous induction process during the first few weeks of September will save you a lot of time later. Writer Bruce Tuckman describes the initial weeks of group development as the 'forming' stage.[4] Every student entering a new classroom at the beginning of the school year is likely to feel some degree of anxiety or uncertainty. Questions at the forefront of their mind might include: 'How will I be treated?' 'How will I fit in?' and 'Will I like this?'

In the forming stage of any group it is essential that you develop a real and felt sense of inclusiveness among the whole group so that all students feel comfortable with each other and are able to take the risks that learning requires. Group induction exercises like the following can be useful.

NAMING EXERCISES

An important first step in getting students to feel more comfortable with one another is by making sure they know each other's names. It's helpful to do this in an open space rather than sitting at desks. Primary teachers often run these naming exercises on the classroom carpet. Secondary teachers might want to put the desks or tables outside the classroom or do these activities in the school hall or canteen.

■ **Neighbours game**

This exercise is best done sitting in a circle. Ask the students to learn the names of the two students sitting either side of them. To begin, the teacher stands in the middle of

---

4 See Appendix 1 for a fuller explanation of Tuckman's group development model.

the circle as 'It'. The teacher chooses a student and says: 'Who are your neighbours?' If a student cannot correctly name both neighbours he or she becomes 'It'.

You can make this game more interesting and fun in this way. If the student does know the name of his neighbours he can either say nothing, choose to become the new 'It' or, more interestingly, call 'new neighbours'. This requires all students to find a new seat, including the current 'It'. The one left without a seat becomes the new 'It' and the game continues until everyone has had plenty of name-learning practice. At the end of the activity or the end of the lesson, ask students whether they now know everyone else's name. If not, they can ask.

■ Self-introductions

If you can't get rid of the tables or desks in your room then simply ask students to stand up and say their name. Ideally, students should come to the front of the class and introduce themselves. It's always a good idea for the teacher to go first. For example: 'My name is Mr Smith. My hobbies are playing rugby, listening to music and playing guitar. I have a wife and two kids.' If students want to volunteer more about themselves than just their name then they can but they should be put under no pressure to do this.

Once the students know each others' names they can start to share information about themselves. Here are some 'getting acquainted' exercises you could try:

■ Describe your partner

Put students into pairs, preferably with a partner they don't know very well. Then ask them to spend up to 10 minutes interviewing each other. They can ask about hobbies, interests, goals, career plans, friends, family and so on. After each person has gathered the information, students can then introduce their partner to the rest of the class. For example: 'My partner Mark supports Everton. He loves running and when he's older he wants to be an astronaut.'

■ The Differences game

Give students whiteboards or ask them to write numbers 1 through to 5 on a separate piece of card or paper. Tell them you are going to ask a series of questions so we can see how people in the class are similar and different. Explain that the reason you are doing this is that you expect the class to work well together and that this activity is a way of helping the students to get to know their classmates. After each question students must rank their preferences on the 1 to 5 scale and notice the score of others so as to be able to get a better understanding of them.

On a flipchart or board write down what the numbers equate to. For example:

---

1 = Yes, very much

2 = Yes, moderately

3 = Undecided or don't want to say

4 = Not really

5 = Not at all

Start with safer questions before moving on to quirkier and more controversial issues:

- How many of you like listening to music?
- How many of you like eating white chocolate?
- How many of you do a lot of chores in the house?
- How many of you enjoy school?
- How many of you think that you should be able to vote when you are 16?

Remember you are using this activity to help get your class better acquainted. When you see an opportunity to show students that they have a similar score for a question you should point this out. Perhaps get students to form a continuum so that they can see who has similar likes, dislikes and opinions. It is also important to stress that those students who have more 'individual' or 'maverick' tastes or opinions are of value too. We don't mean personal views that may be illegal, such as racism, but students who might hold strong views or very unique tastes. Say things like, 'It's brilliant that you have your own style' or 'I like the fact that you don't follow the same approach as others; that shows strong character'.

Red carpet

This game is best played in a room without desks. The red carpet, the kind celebrities walk on at a film premiere, can simply be made from a roll of wallpaper on which you write 'red carpet' or get a remnant from a local carpet shop.

Ask the class for a volunteer to walk the red carpet and be interviewed. The rest of the class can then act as reporters and photographers. As the first volunteer walks the red carpet they can be asked questions that help the students get to know each other. Each student should take it in turn to walk the red carpet for up to two minutes.

This game can be debriefed by the teacher asking students to recall what they've learnt about their fellow classmates. Here are some suggested questions (in case your students can't think of any):

- What are your ambitions?
- Where would you most like to travel in the world?
- What (other) famous person would you most like to meet?
- Who is your hero?
- What is your most treasured possession/favourite toy?

WHOLE CLASS GUIDELINES

Getting your students to develop guidelines for how they will work together should be done in the first few weeks of the school year. Ask them to brainstorm and develop ideas that will support cooperative learning. How might they create an environment where everyone can work together to meet their learning targets and even go beyond them?

Get students to write their suggestions on the board or a flipchart. You might have to prompt them to think about things such as how they treat other people's ideas, how they encourage each other, how they try their best and so on. This works best when all the ideas come from the students so that they have ownership of them. Examples might include things like:

- Don't hurt people's feelings.
- Try our best.
- Work with our teacher to do well.
- Listen to other people's ideas with respect.
- Take turns when speaking.

Once all the ideas are written up, work with your students to summarise them into three to five points and reach consensus through discussion. Teachers will have their own rules but these guidelines should be student generated and must not feel imposed. It is helpful to use phrases such as 'Does everyone agree on that point?' or 'Who can think of a simpler way of phrasing that?' or 'Is there anyone who can't live with that rule because we will be using it all year?' We prefer consensus rather than democracy because *everyone* in the class needs to buy into the rules.

Give every student a copy of the final agreement and ask them to sign it. Explain that a signature on a contract is legally binding. It's also a good idea to have a copy of the agreement on the classroom wall. Invite students with good art skills to make this. Then stress again that these are *their* rules and invite them to police it wherever possible for themselves. These ground rules can become very powerful in encouraging your students to be the best they can be and create powerful and workable social norms that encourage good learning habits.

USING TEAMWORK RUBRICS

Just as the phrase 'try harder' means different things to different students, so does the word 'teamwork'. This is where teamwork rubrics can help. Using such a document for all their teamwork activities enables students to have a better idea of their current level of teamwork skills and what they can do to improve. Teamwork rubrics can be broken down into five areas and four levels. What follows is a brief overview. The full teamwork rubric can be found in Appendix 2.

The five areas are:

1   Focusing on the task.

2   Problem-solving.

3   Research and information sharing.

4   Listening, questioning and discussing.

5   Organisation and work habits.

Each area can be developed separately or in combination with other areas. For example, when developing the skills of your students in the area of *organisation and work habits* this part of the rubric can help them rate their competence and set targets for improvement.

The four levels are:

Level 1 (highest): You play a key part in team planning and you meet every personal target that the team has set you. You meet all deadlines, your attendance is perfect and you always show a positive attitude about the task and working with others. You are completely reliable.

Level 2: You play a part in team planning and you meet most personal targets that the team has set you. You meet most deadlines, your attendance is high and you always show a positive attitude about the task and working with others. You are mostly reliable.

Level 3: You play a small part in team planning and you meet some of your personal targets that the team has set you. You meet most deadlines, your attendance is good and you mostly show a positive attitude about the task and working with others.

Level 4: You play no part in team planning but you do meet some of your personal targets that the team has set you. You are not always reliable.

After the students assess their current level of teamwork they can set themselves targets for improvement. This can also be done by classmates and/or by their teacher.

THE EVALUATION WHEEL

The evaluation wheel is a simple but effective way of getting students to assess their own contribution as well as the contribution of others in their group.

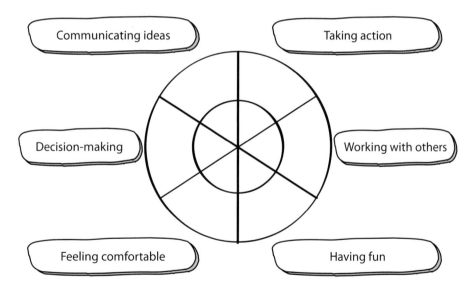

Note: You can download the evaluation wheel template at http://osiriseducational.co.uk/outstandingteaching/resources.

To assess self or others, students should colour in each segment in the inner circle proportionately to show how successfully the indicator was met. Colouring a tip of the wedge represents it being hardly met; colouring the whole wedge represents it being completely met. The outer wedge can then be filled with comments or suggestions for effective change.

An evaluation wheel can be revisited throughout the duration of a project so that improvements can be recorded. For instance, when a self-rated segment goes from low to high (or vice versa) there must be reasons for this. These reasons can be explored and can help students become more skilful in peer and self-assessment.

■ Are you teaching a class who don't get on well as a group? If so, what do you think is holding them back? Lack of clarity about how an effective group should perform? Poor teamwork skills? Lack of rapport between students?

■ How can you induct your next new class thoroughly so that they quickly develop the skills and attitudes to be able to work at high levels of engagement?

Create higher expectations for your class to work as an effective group by using teamwork rubrics, an evaluation wheel, whole class guidelines or group development games.

FAQS

Is it best to try some of these ideas at the beginning of the school year?

Ideally you should use many of these ideas from the first time you meet a class in September. If, however, you are reading this book and you have already started with a class, think about introducing the techniques that will most impact on the students habits. Your choice of whether to start to incorporate stuck boards, effort levels, teamwork rubrics or universal truths into your teaching will depend upon the learning habits that you want to grow in your students. Teachers who are consistently rated as outstanding tend to have a clear sense of what these habits should be.

I've got too much to cover as it is. Why should I try to develop attitudes, skills and habits as well?

It is our assertion that coverage is the enemy of depth. There certainly are ill-devised schemes of work and over-elaborate syllabi out there which might seem to offer little flexibility but it is our job as teachers to help students to achieve their highest potential. Students will only be able to attain the highest grades if they are working at thinking levels towards the top of Bloom's Taxonomy. This is hard to achieve when a teacher has a paradigm of teaching being 'transmitting to' rather than 'exploring with'. Try to keep in mind the acronym KASH. Knowledge such as facts can often be learned without the aid of a teacher but when you develop or transform students' attitudes, skills and habits your teaching will help them to be not only highly engaged in your lessons but have a positive impact beyond your lessons. You could even be the teacher that changed their life.

IN A NUTSHELL

No matter how good a teacher is at getting his or her subject across, effective learning simply will not happen if a class has low engagement and poor learning skills and attitudes. There are only two choices for the teacher when faced with such a situation: accept it the way it is or work to transform the students' attitudes and limiting beliefs. *Training* your class to cope with being stuck, to work cooperatively together and to do their best enables them to spend more time reflecting on how to improve their academic work and develop the 'right' skills and attitudes. This will help them to be more engaged by your teaching and their *own* learning.

FOR MORE INFORMATION ...

Art Costa and Bena Kallick, *Learning and Leading with Habits of Mind: 16 Essential Characteristics for Success* (Alexandria, VA: Association for Supervision and Curriculum Development, 2009)

Jack Canfield and Frank Siccone, *101 Ways to Develop Student Self-Esteem and Responsibility* (Boston, MA: Allyn & Bacon, 1994).

Victor Frankl, *Man's Search for Meaning: The Classic Tribute To Hope from the Holocaust* (London: Random House, 1959).

Ian Gilbert, *Why Do I Need a Teacher When I've Got Google? The Essential Guide to the Big Issues for Every 21st Century Teacher* (London: Routledge, 2010).

Martin Seligman, *Learned Optimism: How to Change Your Mind and Your Life* (New York: Simon & Schuster, 1991).

Gene Stanford, *Developing Effective Classroom Groups* (Oxford: Hart Publishing, 1977).

Chapter 6

I KNOW HOW TO GET OUTSTANDING NOW!

Here is Edward Bear, going upstairs, now, bump, bump, bump, on the back of his head behind Christopher Robin. It is, as far as he knows, the only way of going upstairs, but sometimes he feels there really is another way, if only he could stop bumping for a moment and think of it.

With apologies to A. A. Milne

The daily life of a teacher is extremely hectic. There never seems to be enough time to reflect properly on why a particular lesson went well or badly or how to improve the quality of learning taking place each day. When we do reflect, it often takes place when we are at our most tired, such as is in the staffroom at the end of the day or in the car while driving home.

WHAT'S IN THIS CHAPTER FOR ME?

- Have you ever felt that teaching was constantly like banging your head against a wall or – like Winnie-the-Pooh – the stairs?

- Have you ever wondered if there were accelerated techniques for moving the engagement levels of a class up?

- Are you sometimes puzzled to know what is expected of an 'outstanding' teacher?

Our work with teachers creates that focused reflection time. We know how crucial it is. One teacher we've worked with said, 'I just realised from watching that DVD of my lesson that the limiting factor in the classroom was not the kids, but my fixed mindset about their ability to cope with a more complex challenge.'

Chapter 5 identified key strategies to help your classes to develop the knowledge, attitudes, skills and habits required to work at the highest levels. Yet developing the learning skills of students is only part of the solution to reaching Level 1a/b. Teachers have to change the way they teach; often more than they might at first think.

This chapter will share learning from the accumulated reflections of huge numbers of passionate teachers around the country. These are individuals who have worked hard to make their teaching more effective. The changes they've made have moved the engagement of their classes up levels. Not only that, they've found the changes have led to much greater pleasure and satisfaction in their work. 'I wish I hadn't put in for early retirement now. I'm really enjoying my teaching again' is one of our favourites! And there are hundreds more comments in the same vein.

We'll explore some of the most effective of these changes so that you too can share the tools and strategies they've used to make such great progress. These tools and strategies have been road-tested. They really do work and can be relied on to unlock higher levels of engagement and flow with the students you teach.

WHAT'S THE THINKING BEHIND THIS CHAPTER?

Creating time for teachers to reflect accurately on their craft is a crucial component if we are to improve the quality of teaching and learning in our schools. So much so that we've put it at the core of our Outstanding Teaching Training Intervention (OTTI) programme. As we described earlier in the Introduction, the OTTI programme looks like this:

THE PROCESS

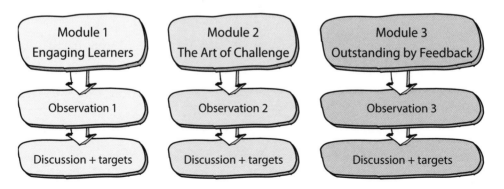

The programme typically runs over two terms. Groups of teachers from a school go through a series of three cycles of training, lesson observation and feedback. Each training session is followed by a videoed observation.

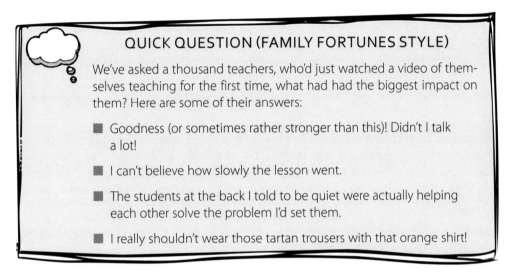

QUICK QUESTION (FAMILY FORTUNES STYLE)

We've asked a thousand teachers, who'd just watched a video of themselves teaching for the first time, what had had the biggest impact on them? Here are some of their answers:

- Goodness (or sometimes rather stronger than this)! Didn't I talk a lot!

- I can't believe how slowly the lesson went.

- The students at the back I told to be quiet were actually helping each other solve the problem I'd set them.

- I really shouldn't wear those tartan trousers with that orange shirt!

The observation provides each teacher with the opportunity to experiment with new techniques and strategies from the training session. After the lesson observation the teacher is presented with a DVD of their lesson. They go home and watch the lesson themselves before meeting with us the following day. We provide them with a set of self-reflection questions to guide their analysis and evaluation of the lesson. A copy of the questionnaire can be found in Appendix 3.

- Have you ever watched yourself teach?

- If not, why not give it a go? Borrow a video camera and ask your teaching assistant (if you have one), a trusted colleague or one of your students to video you teaching a class. Use our self-reflection questions in Appendix 3 and the levels descriptions at the front of the book, to reflect on how the lesson went.

In this meeting we discuss what level the lesson achieved, why it was this level, and, most importantly, how they can move engagement in lessons up from this level.

Watching yourself teach is something the vast majority of teachers have never done before. The prospect can be terrifying for some, but ultimately intriguing for all. Watching yourself teach a lesson opens up a window on an almost parallel world that is recognisable, but strangely different.

For a start, we sound quite different to how we hear ourselves 'live'. And there are other, even more alarming, differences revealed by the positioning of the camera. When we see our lesson from the back of the class rather than the front, the perspective is quite different. This perspective, the students' perspective, actively challenges many of the deeply held perceptions we might have about ourselves as teachers and what really goes on in our classrooms.

This process has brought countless moments of epiphany. These insights can be so powerful that they've permanently transformed the teaching habits of many teachers we've worked with. The experience also provokes a more inquisitive attitude as teachers begin to question more of their other assumptions about what really happens in their classroom: 'If I haven't noticed that my explanations were poor, what other blind spots might I have?'

As R. D. Laing so beautifully put it: 'The range of what we think and do is limited by what we fail to notice. And because we fail to notice that we fail to notice, there is little we can do to change; until we notice how failing to notice shapes our thoughts and deeds.'[1]

Watching ourselves teach helps us to notice what we've been failing to notice. We can only change what we're aware of. And as we become more aware we can also see what we're doing well in addition to what we can improve. For many teachers, noticing how engaged a class are during their experimental lesson and the quality and depth of student–student dialogue, has been a joy to both them and to us. Especially given that they were delightfully redundant at the front of the room when they got their students into flow. These experiences have spurred them on to continue with their modified approach to teaching.

HOW CAN I CHANGE MY TEACHING TO MOVE ENGAGEMENT LEVELS UP?

As in Chapter 5, the KASH (Knowledge, Attitudes, Skills, Habits) model can be invaluable in developing strategies to move up levels. Only once the characteristics of those teachers consistently achieving engagement Level 1a have been identified can we create a personal action plan.

---

1 D. Goleman, in *Vital Lies, Simply Truths: The Psychology of Self-deception* (London: Bloomsbury), p. 24.

▓ Teachers have the 'right' knowledge

Teachers at Level 1a plan in a more effective way than those operating at Level 3. They are clear about the prior knowledge, understanding and skills of their class. They have planned the lesson so that all learners make rapid progress. This will include differentiating the level of challenge. They know their subject well and are constantly seeking to deepen the learning of their students. They also know their class as individuals – understanding which intrinsic motivators engage them – and plan lessons accordingly.

▓ Teachers have the 'right' attitude

Every minute is crucial to these teachers. From the minute the students enter the room no time is wasted. For example, they will have a challenge on the board to get their classes engaged. They are teachers who are risk-takers. They are constantly thinking about how they can improve the quality of their teaching and the learning taking place.

▓ Teachers have the 'right' skills

At Level 1a, teachers are constantly getting feedback from questioning or observation. They are using it to decide what to do next. They have developed the KASH of their classes so that their role has changed to become one of activator and challenger. These teachers have excellent interpersonal skills and use them to engage students.

▓ Teachers have the 'right' habits

At Level 1a, teachers ensure that students lead their learning for significant periods. They have broken the habit of talking too much and habitually get their students to lead their learning.

One PE teacher, Tony Threlkeld, uses a great technique to minimise time between activities. He challenges one student to collect up resources from the completed activity faster than he gives out the resources for the next task. Running is of course banned!

Changing the way we teach means doing things differently. We might need to add skills, put more focus on things we already do, do some things less or stop doing them altogether. The remainder of this chapter provides step-change advice to develop Level 1a teacher KASH.

TALK, TALK, TALK

By far, the most common reflection of teachers who've watched themselves on DVD playback is that they were completely unaware of just how much talking they did during the lesson. And these were lessons they'd planned especially carefully to ensure that students took more ownership than normal! Talking is what teachers do, but too much of it can lead to engagement levels falling off dramatically. It is also the reason why many of us end the term with sore throats and high levels of exhaustion.

Inviting teachers to consider just how much of their talking is strictly necessary has been a valuable exercise for many of them. As a result, they've begun to structure their lessons so that they lead less and their students lead more. Teachers who make this shift frequently find that the change is transformational both for them and for their students.

> Get a stopwatch and time how much of your lesson is devoted to student-led learning. Time how much of the lesson you spend talking. Could you reduce your teacher talk by 10% or even 20% over the next two weeks?

Here are four proven activities that can push learners to lead their own learning. Each activity offers suggestions for application as well as ways to build in differentiation.

CONSENSUS

Resources: Flipchart paper/pens

Consensus is an excellent activity. It provides well-structured group discussion, opportunities for higher order questioning, ways to challenge for deeper understanding and requires little in the way of resources. It's an activity that is suitable for a variety of contexts, for example: situations in which students need to discuss and refine their understanding of a concept, problem or topic; or when they need to apply, analyse or evaluate source evidence or case-study material in order to answer questions such as, 'What were the issues facing Germany in 1930?' Consensus may be used in preparation for work on a past exam paper question, essay or project.

Consensus also works very effectively at the start of a topic to gain feedback from students about what they already know about it. For example, 'What is Fairtrade all about?' This helps the teacher to plan subsequent lessons, ensuring the class are not revisiting aspects of the topic they already understand – a situation which is guaranteed to extinguish flow. It also alerts the teacher to any misconceptions the students may have that will need to be addressed.

How to use: The class are split into groups of four. Each group is given a piece of flipchart paper with a large circle in the middle.

Step 1: The big question is posed to the class. If there is source evidence or case-study material, students may be given 5 to 10 minutes to read and analyse this.

Step 2: Each student, working in silence, writes down their own thoughts about possible answers anywhere on the sheet of paper except for the circle in the middle. Depending on the complexity of the question, students may be given up to 5 minutes to do this.

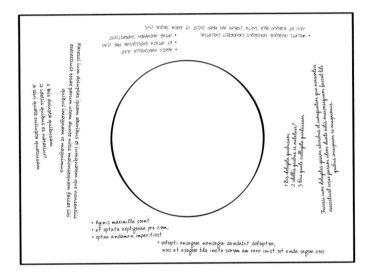

Step 3: At this point the circle in the middle of the paper comes into play. The students are given as long as 15 minutes to discuss their ideas in their group. Whenever agreement is reached, the idea is written in the circle which represents the area of consensus. Only ideas that have unanimous agreement within the group can be written in the circle. This forces students to refine and clarify ideas so that they can all find agreement. It may be helpful for the group to then rank or prioritise the points they have agreed on and/or provide evidence to back them up.

The teacher can provide differentiation by introducing contradictory statements or more complex evidence for abler groups or she can provide definitions and scaffolding for the less able learners. As the teacher circulates, she is likely to find opportunities to challenge students to clarify what they mean or invite them to provide evidence to justify their points. Alternatively, certain groups could be challenged to make causal links between their points of consensus.

Step 4: It is generally useful to invite different groups to share their consensus thoughts with other groups across the class. This can be done in a number of different ways. For example, creating new groups formed from individual members of each of the original groups.

A very useful follow-up activity is Marketplace.

MARKETPLACE

Resources: Flipchart paper/pens

The aim of Marketplace is to provide an opportunity for students to gain deeper understanding of new content through discussion and peer-teaching. If used as a follow-up to Consensus, start at Stage 3 below. Alternatively, different groups might be given one aspect of a new topic to learn about and then peer-teach the rest of the class. Or groups may be given the same scenario as the rest of the class but are asked to explore the situation from the perspective of a particular character or stakeholder. Once the peer-teaching has taken place, the whole class are given a test to provide feedback to the teacher.

Stage 1 (setting up – 5 minutes): Write up the sequence and the timing of each stage on the board so that the class are clear about what they need to do and how long they have to do it. This also impresses upon them the importance of good time management. It is also essential at this stage to outline the content of the test at the end of the activity so that students are clear about the areas on which they should focus their research.

Stage 2 (research – 20 minutes): Each group of a maximum of four students researches their content and is given a time limit of 20 minutes. The group use flipchart paper to create a poster resource that will explain their content to others. It is helpful to impose an upper word limit. We suggest a maximum of 20 words but unlimited drawings, symbols, numbers, cartoons and diagrams are to be encouraged. This encourages the students to translate written information from the research material into visual information on their flipchart page. All of the group should play a part in producing the poster. Each of the class groups will be researching a different element of the topic.

Stage 3 (peer-teaching – 5 minutes): When the time limit is up, one member of the group stays with their poster and takes the role of market trader. Their job is to teach their content to other students in the class using their poster. We strongly advise that they should stand while they do this. One member from each group then visits each of the market traders, making notes about the new content being delivered.

Stage 4 (feedback – 5–10 minutes): Each group then re-forms and they feed back what they have learned from the other market traders to each other. They are encouraged to make links between the information they have learnt from the different market traders.

Stage 5 (test – 10 minutes): To get feedback on the learning that has occurred, give the groups a test or quiz. This can provoke high levels of competition between the groups. Allowing the groups to confer encourages the development of better rapport and communication skills.

LEARNING JIGSAW

This can be a fantastic activity, particularly when students are learning a new skill or when they need to compare and contrast different ideas, concepts and stages/steps in a process. The overarching idea behind the activity is that students teach themselves and then teach others. For example, you may want your History students to explore the statement: 'Evaluate the factors that led to King Harold's defeat at Hastings'. You would set up four workstations in the room ensuring that the information and material at each station is not sufficient to solve the challenge on its own.

Let's use a detailed example from a Year 7 netball lesson that we observed a couple of years ago. The room was laid out with four workstations around the sports hall.

Step 1 (5 minutes): Students were organised into groups of four and numbered themselves as 1, 2, 3 and 4. The teacher then explained the purpose of the lesson and the structure of the activity.

Step 2 (12–15 minutes): The groups split up. All of the number ones went to workstation 1, number twos to workstation 2 and so on. At each workstation there were a set of resources, instructions and success criteria. Using the materials, the students had to teach themselves a particular drill so that they would be confident enough to go back and teach the others in their group as well as give them feedback on the quality of their performance. During this stage, the teacher monitors the groups to ensure that the students at each workstation are progressing well.

Step 3 (20 minutes): The students now return to their 'home' group where they take it in turns to teach each other the particular drill each one has learnt. Again, the teacher's role is to monitor and challenge where appropriate.

Step 4 (10 minutes): The class is brought back together to reflect on the amount of progress made and what mistakes or difficulties were encountered. Findings can be connected to other topics that the students have learnt about previously. It can be a great idea to video the performance of different groups and play these back so that the students can gain greater insights into what they have done well and what they need to improve.

MODELLING THE LEARNING

Resources: varies but could include Play-Doh, card, straws, sand, sieves, water, balloons, food colouring and marbles

Many teachers, particularly those in secondary schools, bemoan their students' perceived lack of creativity. This activity provides opportunities for students to explore and display their ingenuity and creativity in spades. Our observation of a Year 13 Biology lesson amply illustrated this. The teacher presented the class with a range of materials and resources. Each student was given an individual challenge of producing and delivering a presentation to the class. Not only did they have to present on one particular function of the kidney but they also had to create a three-dimensional model to demonstrate their understanding.

They worked independently with very little assistance from the teacher who repeatedly referred any student looking for help back to their notes or to the textbook. After each presentation, the teacher asked questions to challenge the presenter about aspects of their presentation and this generated in-depth conversations between students about the nature and functions of the kidney. Many misconceptions were corrected through this process. The teacher acted merely as a facilitator, using questioning to push the students to further clarify their understanding.

> Consider how you might develop the quality of student–student dialogue using one or more of the strategies above.

PERFORMANCE SKILLS:
BODY LANGUAGE AND RAPPORT

Teaching requires us to be actors. Each lesson involves putting on a performance in every interaction we have with our students. Becoming more aware of how we are perceived by our students can be one of the most challenging elements of self-reflection for teachers. After all, how we look, move and sound are very personal elements.

One teacher viewed her first filmed lesson and bemoaned how miserable she looked: 'I never smiled once!'

We asked: 'Do you get on with the class?' 'Yes, they're my favourite!'

She now has the word 'SMILE' on the back wall of her classroom in big letters. Her classes have no idea why it's there but it serves to remind her about a small but crucial element in making her classroom a more positive learning environment.

Teachers notice many things when they observe themselves on video. Do they smile or not? Are they stuck behind their desk or do they move around the room? Do they distribute their eye contact evenly with all the students? Or do they favour some students over others or prefer the left side of the classroom to the right? All these factors have a significant effect on the quality of rapport a teacher can build with their students.

These and other factors can also significantly affect the enthusiasm a teacher appears to have for their subject and for the value of learning about it. In particular, voice modulation, facial expression and open posture can create an engaging climate and energy in the classroom. After watching her DVD, one teacher in a tough inner-city school said this about her most challenging class: 'I was really pleased that I came across as someone who enjoys teaching these kids, even though I dread the lesson each week – it keeps me awake at night.' If the class perceive she's on their side and enjoying what she does with them, they are much more likely to become engaged and open to the possibilities she offers.

Voice is a particularly important component in the performance skills of the teacher. Used effectively, the pitch and modulation of a teacher's voice can facilitate an engaged classroom. Often, lowering the volume rather than raising it is far more productive as learners strain to listen to instructions. Indeed, one teacher feigned losing her voice so that she could only whisper instructions. As a result the class started to work much more independently. There are many strategies in an outstanding teacher's toolkit – sometimes even deception for a higher purpose can be one!

Get some feedback on your performance skills from colleagues and students:

- Does your voice convey enthusiasm and confidence?

- Is your body language open and confident? Does it convey a sense of purpose?

- Are there areas of your room you subconsciously avoid?

BACKWARD PLANNING

For some teachers better planning provides a real springboard for jumping up levels rapidly. Common examples of poor planning include lack of challenge, little or no differentiation, too much content and the lesson being overly teacher-led. The poorly constructed plans that the inspector was seeing were not the result of lack of effort or commitment on the part of the teachers concerned. The problem was they had not really considered *the desired outcome* of the lesson before they decided on its structure and content. In other words, what they should have used is what we call *backward planning*.

One of Her Majesty's Inspectors commented to us that he could grade the majority of lessons as 'satisfactory' in one particular school simply by reading the lesson plan in advance (see below). He could see immediately that there were structural problems with the plan and that it was doomed at the outset unless the teacher found some way of improvising around the problems that would inevitably arise.

In their book *Understanding by Design*, Grant Wiggins and Jay McTighe argue that planning lessons backwards can provide much greater clarity for both teacher and students.[2] There are three stages in the process:

1   Identify the desired result. What do you want the students to know, understand and be able to do by the end of the lesson or sequence of lessons? This will be a series of differentiated goals for students at different levels of ability.

2   Determine what exactly will demonstrate understanding. What will be acceptable evidence that the class has achieved the desired results outlined in Stage 1?

3   Once the stages above have been decided, the teacher can choose the learning activities that she'll use. These learning activities will generate the evidence required in Stage 2.

(Adapted from *Understanding by Design*)

If the first two stages are not undertaken, it's much less likely that the desired learning outcomes will be met because the activities chosen may not enable students to demonstrate sufficient evidence. On the other hand, starting with a firm grasp of the desired result, as set out in Stage 1, is likely to provoke three key questions:

1   What does progress look like this in this topic?

2   Do the learners know what progress looks like?

3   How can my lesson plan enable this progress to take place?

Teachers can now translate these insights into learning objectives that are specific, challenging, measurable, realistic and time appropriate.

Consider a learning objective stated like this:

---

2 Grant P. Wiggins and Jay McTighe, *Understanding by Design* (Alexandria, VA: Association for Supervision and Curriculum Development, 2005).

Task: Understand the carbon cycle

The inherent vagueness and wide scope of this objective make the task of devising learning activities rather difficult. Additionally, how will the teacher assess progress towards the objective? What would be the evidence that the class are making this progress?

When using the planning backwards method to establish learning objectives, it makes good sense to choose verbs from Bloom's Taxonomy. Thus, the previous learning objective could be set out in this way:

▪ *Identify* the stages in the carbon cycle.

▪ *Apply* knowledge of the carbon cycle to a decaying potato.

▪ *Analyse* the similarities and differences between the stages in the carbon cycle.

Note that the objectives allow opportunities to move up Bloom's Taxonomy, providing the challenge to create flow. When teachers discover the value of backward planning they realise that changes in their schemes of work become inevitable. Rather than lists of content and activities, they will now have a range of student competences they are seeking to develop.

Thus in a Business Studies class we observed, on stages in the recruitment process, the teacher ensured that there were opportunities to really stretch high-ability students. In her plan they had to *apply* their knowledge to different scenarios and *analyse* and *evaluate* the most suitable recruitment processes for different firms. Using this approach, the students were much more likely to develop the skills and attitudes to achieve or exceed their target grade in the examination room. They had not only developed an understanding of the stages in the recruitment process, but were also able to demonstrate the skills of application, analysis and evaluation called for in the exam.

Teachers we've encouraged to plan backwards have noticed several important benefits. They described seeing a marked improvement in the students' understanding of the learning objectives but they also found themselves more conscious of differentiating the learning. It's no surprise to us that they found their classes moved up levels. After all, clear goals and differentiated challenge are two of the foundations for achieving flow.

When asked, 'What would outstanding progress look like in your lesson?', one teacher described our challenge as sparking a moment of epiphany. The teacher had been so focused on the content of the lesson that he hadn't thought about anything else. As a consequence the class hadn't been at all clear about the real goal or purpose. As a result, they had stumbled through the lesson, experimenting with materials as if blindfolded. Learning in this way is rather like attempting a 500-piece jigsaw puzzle without being allowed to look at the picture on the box!

Re-evaluate your lesson planning technique and ask yourself the following questions:

- Do your lesson plans satisfy the three stages in backward planning?

- Is there sufficient challenge and differentiation in the objectives set?

CONCLUSION:
ARE WE READY TO CHANGE OUR MINDSET?

On the surface, much of what we do when working with teachers appears to be about supporting them to take the necessary steps for making learning and teaching outstanding. This may include clarity about the key ingredients, awareness of the relevant pedagogy and practical tools that can be directly applied in the classrooms. However, there is a much more powerful process at work within the Outstanding Teaching Training Interventions programmes that we run.

Teachers who volunteer for the programme – and they always are volunteers – are expected to take risks and try out new things. We always say that the only way you can fail our course is by not taking risks. After all, we learn nothing by playing safe. We require our teachers to try out new learning in their classes and we video them as they do it. We encourage them to watch, reflect on and learn from the feedback they get. We also invite them to demand more feedback from their students. This is particularly challenging for those teachers who don't see the value and power of feedback. It is only feedback that can guide them to make and embed the changes that will help them 'level up' student engagement.

There are the countless individuals we've worked with who've started the programme with the limiting belief that they can't teach outstanding lessons. They have all sorts of reasons and excuses for this: it's too much work; they don't have time; or even that the learners in their class can't cope with working independently. It has been so rewarding to see them prove themselves wrong. At the end of their learning journey they've reflected on the way their mindset has changed. In some cases they've been known to pass around copies of their first and last DVDs so that others can see how their learning has transformed both their own teaching and their students' learning.

We, as teachers, model lots of fantastic norms to our classes such as good timekeeping, politeness and good personal organisation. Yet it could be argued that the most important norm to model with our students is that of being a curious and engaged learner – one who is eager and open to try new things, who seeks feedback to help themselves improve, grow and develop and who is willing to take whatever risks are necessary.

If everyone in the school community were learners, it would provide a culture in which all look to improve. It would be a place where on a day-to-day basis staff and students would be open to feedback and would use this feedback to open themselves to new possibilities in a virtuous cycle of continuous learning and development.

FAQS

How do I know what engagement level I'm at?

Get as much feedback as you can from your students through class surveys, discussions, peer observation and drop-ins from supportive colleagues or your teaching assistant. Best of all, arrange for a lesson to be videoed so you can decide for yourself. Use the self-reflection questionnaire in Appendix 3 to help guide your reflection.

What's the first step to changing?

Imagine the challenges you face as a series of boulders in your path to Level 1a. You can always choose which boulders to navigate your way around first. We would suggest you begin with the quick and easy wins or the ones that are likely to have the biggest and most noticeable impact. Often, getting past one boulder provides the strategies, tools and confidence you need to help shift or go beyond subsequent obstacles.

IN A NUTSHELL

The journey to levelling up engagement started the day you began teaching. Knowing your current level of performance is crucial to developing a plan to move teaching and learning forward – and the best way of establishing this is by watching yourself teach. Good luck and enjoy the learning journey, one level at a time! You are the main model for your students' learning.

FOR MORE INFORMATION ...

Guy Claxton, *What's the Point of School? Rediscovering the Heart of Education* (Oxford: Oneword, 2008).

John Hattie, *Visible Learning for Teachers: Maximizing Impact on Learning* (Abingdon and New York: Routledge, 2011).

If you're looking for more tools for your teaching toolkit, try these two classics:

Paul Ginnis, *The Teacher's Toolkit: Raise Classroom Achievement with Strategies for Every Learner* (Carmarthen: Crown House Publishing, 2001).

Geoff Petty, *Evidence Based Teaching: A Practical Approach*, 2nd edn (Cheltenham: Nelson Thornes, 2009).

If you're struggling to change habits, this book could really help you:

Chip Heath and Dan Heath, *Switch: How To Change Things When Change Is Hard* (London: Random House, 2010).

Are your learners too dependent? This clip will make them laugh out loud with incredulity but they'll probably be able to see how it also relates to their own situation in class:

http://www.youtube.com/watch?v=oXCuGvsThEw.

Appendix 1:

TUCKMAN'S GROUP DEVELOPMENT MODEL

In 1965, Dr Bruce Tuckman created a group development model known as Forming–Storming–Norming–Performing. His model charts the different stages teams must go through in order to become effective.

Many things must happen as a team matures. Better relationships will become established within the group and the leader's role will change too. In particular, the leader will shift from a directive style to a coaching role, finally becoming more of a participating colleague. By this time, the leader's role is mainly to encourage direction and vision and to delegate tasks and duties. The group will be pretty well leading themselves.

Tuckman's model was developed primarily with business and professional organisations in mind but has clear relevance for learning environments. The model shows how step by step we can influence individuals to move from a situation where they are far from working at their best, to becoming an effective and collaborative group where all are making rapid individual and collective progress.

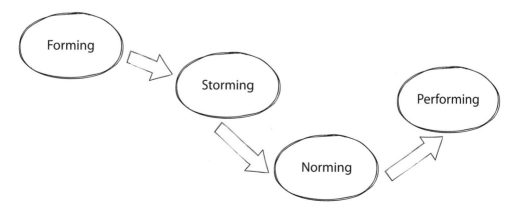

The diagram above shows our interpretation of Tuckman's model. After the initial forming there will always be a storming stage: a time of resistance and challenge. However, once this stage is successfully navigated then the norming and performing stages are possible to reach.

STAGE 1: FORMING

When a student enters a new classroom with other people there may be anxiety and uncertainty. They will be asking themselves questions such as 'How will I be treated?', 'How will I fit in?' and 'Will I like this?' The students are forming their opinions of the environment, the subject and the teacher.

Behaviours of the group: talkative, polite, anxious, teacher-dependent.

Output of group: low productivity.

Teacher's role: the teacher directs at this stage – organising, setting ground rules and establishing standards.

STAGE 2: STORMING

As students get used to a teacher and become accustomed to working with their classmates, it would seem logical that they would be less likely to get involved in conflict; but in reality the opposite is true. It seems there is a primeval need for humans to assert themselves and test conventional boundaries. The amount of time that a class spends at this stage will depend largely on how well the teacher handles the process.

Behaviours of the group: disagreements, resistance, hostility, defensiveness.

Output of group: low productivity.

Teacher's role: the teacher sells the benefits of the learning, works hard to create consensus and encourages students to find ways to manage conflict and take greater responsibility for themselves, their behaviours and their social interactions.

STAGE 3: NORMING

The norming stage is crucial to the group's growth. It is the period when individuals learn to organise themselves into effective teams by establishing and maintaining social norms that support successful cooperation. However, in the early development of this stage they may struggle with issues of power and responsibility. Who is important and who is not? What are the best procedures for decision making? To what extent will the group consider and include a person with dissenting opinions?

Although the forming stage of group development may have gone well, being well acquainted isn't enough to ensure success as a working group. Many students are not familiar with the skills and attitudes that are required for productive group work. This is because the norms and procedures in the average classroom are generally based upon the students focusing on the instructions of the teacher. At this stage, the teacher will need to introduce these skills and strategies to the learners. They will need to let go of the need to control and develop a more participative culture in the classroom.

Behaviours of the group: comfortable, sharing ideas, cooperative, conflicts minimised and often successfully resolved, harmony, enjoyment.

Output of group: moderate to high.

Teacher's role: nurturing, coaching, affirming, encouraging.

STAGE 4: PERFORMING

At this stage a real group identity emerges. The group becomes increasingly effective, both at accomplishing tasks and in meeting the emotional needs of its members. Cohesiveness is very high. Problems do crop up but the group uses and improves its skills and collective wisdom in dealing with them.

This is what the struggle has all been about. The group has become a well-functioning unit. There may be temporary regressions and occasional temptations to focus more on inter-group relationships than getting tasks done, but a little gentle persuasion is usually enough to get the students back on track.

Once a class has developed into a productive, performing and well-formed group, the range of learning activities that can be satisfactorily and successfully undertaken widens considerably. This stage is marked by a visible and tangible sense of engagement, flow and pleasure in learning experiences both for the students and their teacher.

Behaviours of the group: open, experimental, intrinsically motivated, flexible.

Output of group: very high.

Teacher's role: supporting, delegating, mentoring.

Appendix 2:

TEAMWORK RUBRIC

Category	Level 1	Level 2	
Focus on the task	As a group member there is evidence that you stay on task all of the time without any reminders. There is clear evidence that as a member of the team you have made the completion of the task a high priority and that you are planning for a successful, high-quality outcome (i.e., you have contributed to the team's goal).	As a group member you mostly stay on task without any reminders. You work hard to complete the task and you are able to plan for a successful outcome (i.e., you have contributed to the team's goal).	
Problem-solving	As a member of the team you always actively seek solutions to problems. You are not afraid to ask the teacher for advice and you show initiative before you do this, such as trying hard to think of your own ideas. You show enthusiasm for solving problems.	As a member of the team you mostly seek solutions to problems. You ask the teacher for advice and you show initiative, such as trying hard to think of your own ideas. You show some interest in solving problems.	

Level 3	Level 4
As a group member you stay on task but you often have to be reminded to work harder. You do show that you can sometimes focus on the task but your concentration can also often be lost. When you do think about the task you do, try to think about how it can be done well.	As a group member you rarely stay on task and you often have to be reminded to work harder. Your concentration on the task is low and you rarely show that you are thinking about how the task can be completed well.
As a member of the team you sometimes seek solutions to problems. You only sometimes show interest in solving problems. You play a small role in your team in terms of problem-solving.	As a member of the team you rarely seek solutions to problems. You show little interest in solving problems and tend to leave this to other members of the group.

Category	Level 1	Level 2
Research and information sharing	As a member of the team you demonstrate that you have gathered an extensive amount of information through a variety of research sources. You play a leading role in sharing, summarising and discussing this information.	As a member of the team you demonstrate that you have gathered information through a variety of research sources. You help to share and discuss this information.
Listening, questioning and discussion	As a team member you always listen to others and ask questions to help to solve problems. You fully contribute to all discussions and show a high degree of respect for other members of your team. You cooperate consistently.	As a team member you mostly listen to others and ask questions to help to solve problems. You contribute to some discussions and show some respect for other members of your team. You cooperate most of the time.
Organisation and work habits	You play a key part in team planning and you meet every personal target that the team has set you. You meet all deadlines, your attendance is perfect and you always show a positive attitude about the task and working with others. You are completely reliable.	You play a part in team planning and you meet most personal targets that the team has set you. You meet most deadlines, your attendance is high and you always show a positive attitude about the task and working with others. You are mostly reliable.

Level 3	Level 4
As a member of the team you demonstrate that you have gathered information through some research sources. You share and discuss some of this information.	As a member of the team you have gathered little if any information through research. You help to discuss the information that has been gathered by other group members.
As a team member you sometimes listen to others and sometimes ask questions to help solve problems. You contribute to some discussions but cooperation is rarely evident.	As a team member you only sometimes listen to others and only sometimes ask questions to help to solve problems. You rarely contribute to discussions and cooperation with other team members is not really evident.
You play a small part in team planning and you meet some of your personal targets that the team has set you. You meet most deadlines, your attendance is good and you mostly show a positive attitude about the task and working with others.	You play no part in team planning but you do meet some of your personal targets that the team has set you. You are not always reliable.

Self-assessment
(your level for teamwork)

Reasons:

Peer-assessment
(your level for teamwork
from a classmate)

Reasons:

Teacher assessment
(your level for teamwork
from your teacher)

Reasons:

Ideas for improving teamwork (Self)

Ideas for improving teamwork (Peer)

Ideas for improving teamwork (Teacher)

Appendix 3:

DVD SELF-REFLECTION QUESTIONS

Please answer the following questions whilst watching the DVD of your lesson.

Engaging learners

What do you *notice* about the engagement of your class? Are they in *flow*? Plot the engagement of your whole class for the duration of your DVD.

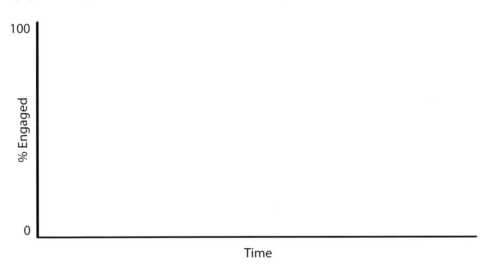

How are you seeking feedback from learners about how interested they are in the learning? Evidence:

How are you using intrinsic motivators (e.g., challenge, curiosity, fun) to raise the engagement levels of your class? Evidence:

Did you use any brain breaks or 3-minute motivators to raise engagement?

What routines are you using to get more whole-class engagement (e.g., discussion guidelines, cooperative norms)? Evidence:

What are you doing to build rapport with individuals in your class? Evidence:

How are you using your performance skills (e.g., body language and voice) to engage learners? Evidence:

What do you think your level was for this lesson (see engaging learners levels)? Evidence:

If you taught this lesson again, what would you do the same and what would you do differently?

BIBLIOGRAPHY

Anderson, L. W. and Krathwohl, D. (eds) (2001). *A Taxonomy for Learning, Teaching and Assessing: A Revision of Bloom's Taxonomy of Educational Objectives*. New York: Longman.

Bowkett, S. (2007). *100+ Ideas for Teaching Creativity* (Continuum One Hundred). London: Continuum.

Bowkett, S. (2007). *100+ Ideas for Teaching Thinking Skills* (Continuum One Hundred). London: Continuum.

Canfield, J. and Siccone, F. (1994). *101 Ways to Develop Student Self-Esteem and Responsibility*. Boston, MA: Allyn & Bacon.

Claxton, C. (1997). *Hare Brain, Tortoise Mind: Why Intelligence Increases When You Think Less*. London: Fourth Estate.

Claxton, G. (2008). *What's the Point of School? Rediscovering the Heart of Education*. Oxford: Oneword.

Costa. A and Kallick B. (2009). *Learning and Leading with Habits of Mind: 16 Essential Characteristics for Success*. Alexandria, VA: Association for Supervision and Curriculum Development

Covey, S. (1989). *The 7 Habits of Highly Effective People*. London: Simon & Schuster.

Csikszentmihalyi, M. (1975). *Beyond Boredom and Anxiety: Experiencing Flow in Work and Play*. San Francisco, CA: Jossey-Bass.

Csikszentmihalyi, M. (1990). *Flow: The Psychology of Optimal Experience*. New York: Simon & Schuster.

Fisher, R. (1997). *Games for Thinking*. Buckingham: Nash Pollock Publishing.

Forehand, M. (2008). *Bloom's Taxonomy: From Emerging Perspectives on Learning, Teaching and Technology*. Available at http://projects.coe.uga.edu/epltt/index.php?title=Bloom%27s_Taxonomy (accessed 12 June 2012).

Frankl, V. (1959). *Man's Search for Meaning: The Classic Tribute To Hope from the Holocaust*. London: Random House (first published in German in 1946 under the title *Ein Psycholog erlebt das Konzentrationslager*).

Gardner, H. (1983). *Frames of Mind: The Theory of Multiple Intelligences*. New York: Basic Books.

Gilbert, I. (2002) *Essential Motivation in the Classroom*. London: Routledge.

Gilbert, I. (2010). *Why Do I Need a Teacher When I've Got Google? The Essential Guide to the Big Issues for Every 21st Century Teacher*. London: Routledge.

Ginnis, P. (2001). *The Teacher's Toolkit: Raise Classroom Achievement with Strategies for Every Learner*. Carmarthen: Crown House Publishing.

Gladwell, M. (2000).*Tipping Point: How Little Things Can Make a Big Difference*. London: Abacus.

Gladwell, M. (2008). *Outliers: The Story of Success*. London: Penguin.

Goleman, D. (1996). *Emotional Intelligence: Why It Can Matter More Than IQ*. London: Bloomsbury.

Goleman, D. (1998). *Vital Lies, Simply Truths: The Psychology of Self-deception*. London: Bloomsbury.

Hattie, J. (2003). *Distinguishing Expert Teachers from Novice and Experienced Teachers. Teachers Make a Difference: What is the Research Evidence?* University of Auckland, Australian Council for Educational Research, October 2003. Available at http://www.acer.edu.au/documents/Hattie_TeachersMakeADifference.pdf (accessed 12 June 2012).

Hattie, J. (2009). *Visible Learning: A Synthesis of Over 800 Meta-Analyses Relating to Achievement*. Abingdon and New York: Routledge.

Hattie, J. (2011). *Visible Learning for Teachers: Maximizing Impact on Learning*. Abingdon and New York: Routledge.

Heath, C. and Heath, D. (2010). *Switch: How To Change Things When Change Is Hard*. London: Random House.

Johnstone, K. (1979). *Impro: Improvisation and the Theatre*. London: Faber and Faber.

Kane, P. (2004). *The Play Ethic: A Manifesto for a Different Way of Living*. London: Macmillan.

Lombard, G. (2003). *Motivational Triggers: Motivating the Disaffected*. Trowbridge: Lifetime Careers.

Ofsted (2012). *The Framework for School Inspection from January 2012*, 30 March 2012. Ref: 090019. Available at http://www.ofsted.gov.uk/resources/framework-for-school-inspection-january-2012 (accessed 12 June 2012).

Owen, N (2001). *The Magic of Metaphor*. Carmarthen: Crown House Publishing.

Owen, N (2004). *More Magic of Metaphor*. Carmarthen: Crown House Publishing.

Owen, N (2009). *The Salmon of Knowledge*. Carmarthen: Crown House Publishing.

Paterson, K. (2007). *3 Minute Motivators: More Than 100 Simple Ways to Reach, Teach and Achieve More Than You Ever Imagined*. Markham, ON: Pembroke Publishers.

Perkins, D. (1992). *Smart Schools: From Training Memories to Educating Minds*. New York: Free Press.

Petty, G. (2009). *Evidence Based Teaching: A Practical Approach*, 2nd edn. Cheltenham: Nelson Thornes.

Petty, G. (2009). *Teaching Today: A Practical Guide*, 4th edn. Cheltenham: Nelson Thornes.

Rogers, C. (1961). *On Becoming a Person: A Therapist's View of Psychotherapy*. London: Constable and Co.

Seligman, M. (1991). *Learned Optimism: How to Change Your Mind and Your Life*. New York: Simon & Schuster.

Stanford, G. (1977). *Developing Effective Classroom Groups*. Oxford: Hart Publishing.

Sutton-Smith, B. (1997). *The Ambiguity of Play*. Cambridge, MA: Harvard University Press.

Wiggins, G. P. and McTighe, J. (2005). *Understanding by Design*. Alexandria, VA: Association for Supervision and Curriculum Development.

ACTIVITIES

INDEX

OSIRIS
EDUCATIONAL

Osiris Educational is the UK's leading independent provider of professional development for teachers.

Osiris believes that every child should receive a world class education. Helping teachers in their continuous development is the crucial step to achieving this. We work at the forefront of innovation in education providing pioneering, challenging and effective training solutions.

More than 200 presenters work with Osiris Educational to help teachers improve their ways of thinking and their approaches to teaching.

Some of the most renowned trainers from across the world work with Osiris Educational including: Professor John Hattie, Professor Barry Hymer, Bill Rogers, Professor Sonia Blandford and Professor Viviane Robinson.

Our 5 crucial paths to CPD training cover everything from Early Years through to Key Stage Five.

Day Courses:
- Leadership and Management
- Teaching and Learning
- Pastoral and Behavioural
- SEN and Gifted and Talented
- Curriculum
- Ofsted

In-School Training:
- Early Years
- Primary
- Secondary

Teacher and Leadership Programmes:
- Outstanding Teaching Intervention
- Leadership Away Days
- Osiris Leader Programme

Conferences and Keynotes:
- Leading Speakers
- Key Issues and Policies

Fast Updates:
- Twilights
- Policy Briefings

FOR MORE INFORMATION CALL 0808 160 5 160
OR VISIT OSIRISEDUCATIONAL.CO.UK